GOD'S SURPRISE

Susan Gately is a freelance journalist, specialising in social, family and religious affairs. A former solicitor, she gave up law to study journalism and spent five years as editor of the online Catholic news service, ciNews. She writes for a number of newspapers, including the *Irish Independent*, *Irish Catholic* and the *Universe*, and does multi-media reports for *Catholic News Service* in Washington.

# GOD'S SURPRISE

## THE NEW MOVEMENTS IN THE CHURCH

SUSAN GATELY

VERITAS

Published 2012 by
Veritas Publications
7–8 Lower Abbey Street
Dublin 1, Ireland
publications@veritas.ie
www.veritas.ie

ISBN 978 1 84730 395 0

10 9 8 7 6 5 4 3 2 1

Shorter versions of the chapters of this book originally appeared as
articles in *Reality* magazine and appear by kind permission of the
editor.

A catalogue record for this book is available from the British Library.

Designed by Heather Costello, Veritas Publications
Printed in the Republic of Ireland by Hudson Killeen Ltd, Dublin

Veritas books are printed on paper made from the wood pulp of managed
forests. For every tree felled, at least one tree is planted, thereby renewing
natural resources.

# Contents

# ≡ Introduction ≡

# God's Surprise: The Ecclesial Movements

'We all need one another'
*St Bernard of Clairvaux*

## Church Crisis

MANY SEE THE CATHOLIC CHURCH TODAY AS BEING in crisis. In twentieth-century Ireland, the Church went from holding a position of power and influence to accelerated contraction as it suffered the onslaught of years of public criticism and humiliation over its appalling handling of sex abuse cases by clergy.

The crisis provoked Pope Benedict XVI to write a pastoral letter to the Catholics of Ireland in March 2010, in which he tried to explain the reason for the failures that had 'such tragic consequences in the lives of victims and their families, and have obscured the light of the Gospel to a degree that not even centuries of persecution succeeded in doing'.[1] The Church in Ireland also faced the challenge of secularisation and the decline in religious practice, he said, pointing to the need for new ways and a new vision.

In fact religious practice in Ireland, while still being high by European standards, has fallen sharply since 1974 when

---

1. Pastoral Letter of the Holy Father Pope Benedict XVI to the Catholics of Ireland, 19 March 2010.

the first reliable records of Mass attendance had 91 per cent of the population at weekly Mass.[2] In 2011, that figure was at 48 per cent and Archbishop Martin said he believed in Dublin it was much lower, at perhaps 20 per cent.[3]

In 2012, a poll by the Association of Catholic Priests found that many baptised Catholics did not hold with key tenets of their Catholic faith, rejecting traditional teachings on sexuality and supporting married and women priests.[4] A large majority believed that divorced or separated people in steady second relationships should be allowed to receive communion.[5]

A Church in crisis? No wonder Archbishop Martin told *60 Minutes* on 4 March 2012, that the Church was reaching 'breaking point'.[6]

**Another Face**
However, operating below the media radar, and much in evidence at the Eucharistic Congress in Dublin in 2012, lies another face of the Catholic Church in Ireland. People who, although horribly upset by the horrendous revelations, are not thrown off course by the storm of criticism and the unrelenting castigations of the Church to which they belong. Many of these people are in ecclesial movements. 'There have always been times when the Church gets into great difficulty, but they can

2. The Lennon et al. report in 1974.

3. Archbishop Diarmuid Martin at the Dublin Diocesan Liturgical Resource Centre Spring Seminar 2011, Holy Cross College, Clonliffe, 5 February 2011.

4. *Contemporary Catholic Perspectives*, commissioned by the Association of Catholic Priests, February 2012.

5. 87 per cent favouring married priests, 77 per cent favouring women priests, 87 per cent in favour of communion for those in second unions.

6. Archbishop of Dublin, Dr Diarmuid Martin, on *60 Minutes*, CBS: 'It [the Catholic Church in Ireland] has reached breaking point. It's at a very difficult stage.'

become times of reform and change,' says Bridie Clancy
from the Cells System of Evangelisation. 'I have hope and
I invoke the Holy Spirit for the future of the Church. We
do not have anything to fear.'

Father Hugh Kavanagh, a priest involved in Focolare,
sees the face of Jesus on the cross in the current dark
moment for the Church. 'This collapse of everything
gives me a new understanding of him. When he cried
out "Why?" he experienced total failure, the apparent
collapse of his mission. Embracing this experience makes
me believe that we can contribute to a new dawn, a new
resurrection, a new life for the Church in Ireland.'

It is a 'time of purification,' says Maura Garrihy from
Youth 2000. 'The Church is about more than those few
priests who abused. I've met the most beautiful priests.
It saddens me to think they're getting the backlash. I've
experienced the Church's vitality and love. The Church
loves you. I couldn't be more determined to show and
share this with others.'

These people could perhaps be compared to the child
who found himself on a ship in the midst of a raging
storm. All those around him were terrified. They were
sure the ship was about to founder. How could it be that
the child was so serene? They asked him 'Aren't you afraid
that we are going to sink?' 'No,' replied the child, 'because
my dad is the captain.'

What strikes you when you meet members of ecclesial
movements is how vibrant their faith is. You can see they
are not just sacramentalised, but evangelised Christians
who belong to small communities. They are turned on to
faith and live what St Paul said: 'When I am weak, then I
am strong.'[7]

---

7. 2 Corinthians 12:10.

## What are the Ecclesial Movements?

The ecclesial movements have been around for a long time. The Irish-established Legion of Mary dates right back to the foundation of the state, and in the course of the twentieth century over one hundred ecclesial movements were born in the Catholic Church, and hundreds more in other Christian Churches.

Before he became Pope Benedict XVI, Cardinal Ratzinger warned against trying to put 'too strict a definition' on the ecclesial movements, for 'the Holy Spirit always has surprises in store and only in retrospect do we realise that the movements have a common essence in the midst of their great diversities.'[8]

He himself became conscious of them in the 1970s when he was a professor of theology in Germany:

> It was a wonderful event for me personally when I came into closer contact with movements such as the Neocatecumenate, Communion and Liberation and Focolare and experienced the energy and enthusiasm with which they lived the faith and were impelled by their joy in it to share with others the gift they had received.

It was a time, said Cardinal Ratzinger, when Karl Rahner and others were speaking of a 'winter in the Church' after the flowering of the Council. He went on:

> But suddenly here was something that no one had planned. Here the Holy Spirit himself had, so to speak, taken the floor. The faith was reawakening precisely

---

8. Cardinal Joseph Ratzinger, 'The Ecclesial Movements: A Theological Reflection on their Place in the Church', in Pontifical Council for the Laity, *Movements in the Church* (Vatican City, 1999).

among the young, who embraced it without ifs, ands or buts, without escape hatches and loopholes, and who experienced it in its totality as a precious, life-giving gift.[9]

Cardinal Ratzinger explained to the World Congress of Ecclesial Movements in 1999 how these movements (which were a 'gift to and in the whole of the Church') fitted into the Catholic Church. Generally, though not always, they derived their origin from a 'charismatic leader' and took shape in 'concrete communities inspired by the life of their founder; they attempt to live the Gospel anew, in its totality, and recognise the Church without hesitation as the ground of their life without which they could not exist.'[10]

The essential criteria for these 'apostolic movements' was that they were rooted in the faith of the Church, and therefore willing to 'stand by the successors of the apostles and the successors of Peter'. They were missionary in spirit, proclaiming the Gospel. 'But this proclamation never happens through words alone; love, which is its inner centre, at one and the same time the centre of its truth and of its action, must be lived and in this way be proclamation. Thus social service is always connected in one form or another with evangelisation.'[11] He went on: 'All of this presupposes – and the source is usually the flame of the initial charism – a deep personal encounter with Christ.'[12]

---

9. Ibid.
10. Ibid.
11. Ibid.
12. Ibid.

In the Catholic Church, the groups are more accurately called 'ecclesial movements' rather than 'lay movements' (even though the vast majority of their members are lay people) by virtue of the fact that they include bishops, priests and religious. 'In so doing they reflect the whole Church,' comments Brendan Leahy, author of *Ecclesial Movements and Communities*.[13]

## Pentecost 1998

The force of these movements first became manifest when they came together at Pentecost 1998 at the invitation of Pope John Paul II. Three hundred thousand members of at least fifty-six different movements/communities gathered in St Peter's Square in an atmosphere of extraordinary joy, as the different groups rejoiced in their own and each others' charisms. Present that day in St Peter's were a number of the prophetic leaders who offered their testimony to the pope and to those present: Chiara Lubich (founder of Focolare), Msgr Luigi Giussani (founder of Communion and Liberation), Kiko Argüello (founder of the Neocatechumenal Way), and Jean Vanier, founder of L'Arche.

In his address, Pope John Paul II said the institutional and charismatic or prophetic aspects of the Church were 'co-essential'. 'They contribute, although differently, to the life, renewal and sanctification of God's people. It is from this providential rediscovery of the Church's charismatic dimension that, before and after the Council, a remarkable pattern of growth has been established for ecclesial movements and new communities.'[14]

---

13. *Ecclesial Movements and Communities* (New York: New City Press, 2011).

14. Pope John Paul II, 30 May 1998. For text, see Pontifical Council for the Laity, *Movements in the Church*, pp. 219–24.

Now there was a new stage for the movements, said John Paul II, the stage of 'ecclesial maturity' where they had to bring forth the more 'mature' fruits of communion and commitment 'that the Church expects from you'. He saw in the movements an answer to the plight of a 'secularised culture' which promotes models of life 'without God', where faith is sorely tested and 'is frequently stifled and dies'.

For John Paul II, the movements were a providential answer to the crisis of faith in the modern world. Groups coming from charisms of the Holy Spirit, with members grounded in a real understanding of their faith, would evangelise their contemporaries.

> Thus we see an urgent need for powerful proclamation and solid, in-depth Christian formation. There is so much need today for mature Christian personalities, conscious of their baptismal identity, of their vocation and mission in the Church and in the world! There is great need for living Christian communities! And here are the movements and the new ecclesial communities: they are the response, given by the Holy Spirit, to this critical challenge at the end of the millennium. You are this providential response.[15]

### The Wave Goes Ecumenical

In the years following the historic gathering of Pentecost 1998, around 200 congresses of movements met locally all over the world, including one in Dublin in 1999 which brought together 1,200 members of movements present in Ireland.

---

15. Ibid., p. 222.

That same year, the progress towards greater union between movements in the Catholic Church became an ecumenical wave, when organisers of Catholic and evangelical movements met in Ottmaring near Augsburg in Germany. The meeting took place immediately after the historic signing of a joint declaration between the Catholic and Lutheran Churches, which agreed a common understanding of the doctrine of Justification, which was at the root of the Protestant Reformation.[16]

A new relationship flourished between them, leading to public rallies and meetings. In a rally in Munich Cathedral on 8 December 2001, for example, members of forty-five movements, communities and groups of the Catholic and Evangelical Church and the Free Churches made a pact that they would love one another the way Christ loved his disciples and that this would form the basis of their communion. Together they decided to work to give a Christian soul to Europe. The action became known as 'Together for Europe' and major gatherings uniting hundreds of movements and communities of the Catholic, Protestant and Evangelical churches have taken place since then, notably in 2004 and 2007 in Germany, and more recently in Belgium. In May 2012, members of three hundred Christian movements and communities of different churches gathered in Brussels to launch a manifesto on the theme of European unity, based on Christian values.

Returning to the situation of the Catholic Church, in 2006 the Vatican published a directory of *International Associations of the Faithful of the Catholic Church*, which listed 122 of these ecclesial movements/communities that

16. *The Joint Declaration on the Doctrine of Justification* by the Lutheran World Federation and the Catholic Church, signed on Reformation Day, 31 October 1999.

have been approved by the Church. Not all are present in Ireland, but quite a number of them are.[17]

## International Linkage and Support

Most of the groups are international, with networks stretching across the globe. The link with their wider international families is particularly strong in groups like Focolare, Communion and Liberation (CL) and the Sword of the Spirit Communities, and this is a powerful support to them. International gatherings, like the huge *Friendship Among Peoples* meeting organised by CL[18] or the Focolare's Genfest[19] draw people from the same movement together from all over the world, reinforcing their particular identity and strengthening their faith.

While a number of movements are very distinctive, coming from a precise founder and charism,[20] a whole collection of communities and movements grew out from Charismatic Renewal – like the Sword of the Spirit (Covenant Communities) and the Cell System of Evangelisation and Youth 2000, not to mention hundreds more individual communities in the Catholic and other Christian Churches. But even so there is something new and vital in each group.

---

17. See appendix, p. 111.

18. An annual week-long meeting in August in Rimini, Italy. In 2011, 800,000 people passed through the festival, which is like a huge expo of the Catholic Church and culture.

19. A festival for young adults. The most recent took place in Budapest in 2012 for 12,000 young people.

20. Like Legion of Mary from Frank Duff (1921), Teams of Our Lady from Fr Henri Caffarel (1939), Focolare from Chiara Lubich (1943), Cursillo from Eduardo Bonnin (1944), Communion and Liberation from Fr Luigi Giussani (1954), L'Arche from Jean Vanier (1964), the Neocatechumenal Way from Kiko Arguello (1964) and Sant'Egidio Community from Andrea Riccardi (1968).

### The Place of Movements in the Church

How movements fit into the life of the Church – either at its centre in the Vatican, or in local parishes – can at times be a topic that causes tension. Back in 1998, when the then Cardinal Ratzinger was being asked to define precisely where they fitted in, he was loath to give an answer. Some movements have priests, religious sisters and even bishops involved in them, and yet at the moment in the Vatican's Curial structures, the movements come under the Pontifical Council for the Laity. Cardinal Ratzinger's reply in 2000 was, 'The question will have to be determined one day. I think that organisation must follow life. It is better therefore to see how life evolves, without rushing to tackle the organisational questions.'[21]

Some movements are very involved in the lives of their local parishes, like the Legion of Mary, where the members, following the instruction of their founder, Frank Duff, are the reliable support of the parish priest. The Cells System of Evangelisation is also parish-based, with members involved in all parish ministries. Focolare has a branch devoted to renewing parish life (Parish Movement) and its members, like those of other groups – Teams of Our Lady, Charismatic Renewal and Cursillo – tend to be very involved in their local parishes, depending on availability and circumstances.

When he was asked about the positive incorporation of movements into parishes in 2000, Cardinal Ratzinger said, 'It is not possible to give a recipe' for this to happen. 'If the persons – the parish priest, the groups and also the bishop – are amenable, solutions will be found.'[22] On that occasion he emphasised once again that bishops must

---

21. Pontifical Council for the Laity, the Ecclesial Movements in the Pastoral Concern of Bishops (Vatican City, 2000), p. 230.
22. Ibid.

consider the gifts that these groups bring to the Church but they also had to 'help the movements to find the right road ... with the responsibility for peaceful harmony within the Church.'[23]

The main thing for the institutional Church is not to stifle the charismatic/prophetic Church. As Benedict XVI said in 1998: 'It must not be the case that everything has to fit into a single, uniform organisation. Better less organisation and more spirit!'[24] He also encouraged movements to be more integrated in the overall pastoral plan of a diocese.

For its part, the 'charismatic' Church has to remain anchored to the magisterium, as Pope Benedict XVI told the young people in Cologne at World Youth Day in 2005, just months after he was elected pope. There he encouraged the young people to get involved in the new movements, but to make sure they were in communion with the bishops and himself. 'It is important to preserve communion with the Pope and with the Bishops. It is they who guarantee that we are ... living in God's great family, founded by the Lord through the Twelve Apostles.'[25]

### The Movements and Religious Vocations

The movements have an attraction for young people, and as such may be viewed as seedbeds for religious vocations. All of these groups awaken faith and undoubtedly foster vocations to the priesthood and religious life. Look into the formative years of a person in religious life, and you will likely find a connection with one group or other

---

23. Ibid.

24. Cardinal Joseph Ratzinger, 'The Ecclesial Movements: A Theological Reflection on their Place in the Church', in Pontifical Council for the Laity, *Movements in the Church* (Vatican City, 1999).

25. Homily at the Mass at Marienfeld (Cologne), Sunday, 21 August 2005.

– Charismatic Renewal or Legion of Mary, Cursillo or Focolare. More recently, Youth 2000 has provided a steady stream of men willing to test out a vocation to religious life.

Some movements have within them strong, fully involving vocations similar to religious vocations, where people are called by God to leave everything and live a life of community, observing the evangelical counsels, but within the framework of a modern spirituality. Such vocations exist in CL, the Sword of the Spirit and Focolare. In some groups entire families put themselves at the disposition of the charism (like L'Arche, Focolare or the Neocatechumenal Way), but to focus on these 'vocations' is, in a way, to miss the point. In the movements, each person sees his or her self as trying to give everything to God, each in his or her own measure. 'Everybody is committed to the fullness of Christian life,' says Pat Johnson from the Community of Nazareth.

The movements unleash the vocation of the laity in the world. As Brendan Leahy writes: 'The movements can be a true leaven in society by promoting a full humanism that finds its measure in the person of Jesus Christ. The life of communion and co-responsibility that movements live can permeate civil society, providing a creative and critical resource for the participative praxis of democracy. And that too can be evangelisation.'[26]

Since he became pope in 2005, Benedict XVI has continued his enthusiastic endorsement of movements as a vital source of life within the Church, and as movements of holiness. Facing the scandal of the horrendous sin and crime of child abuse and calls for reform in the Church,

---

26. Leahy, *Ecclesial Movements and Communities* (New York: New City Press, 2011), p. 118

he has recognised, like Pope John Paul II, that authentic renewal comes from holiness.

'You could say, "the Church has need of these great currents, movements and witnesses of holiness ... but there are none!" In this regard, I confess to you the pleasant surprise that I had in making contact with the movements and the new ecclesial communities', he told bishops at Fatima in 2010. 'Watching them, I had the joy and grace to see how, at a moment of weariness in the Church, at a time when we were hearing about "the winter of the Church", the Holy Spirit was creating a new springtime, awakening in young people and adults alike, the joy of being Christian, of living in the Church, which is the living Body of Christ. Thanks to their charisms, the radicality of the Gospel, the objective contents of the faith, the living flow of her tradition, are being experienced in a persuasive way and welcomed as a personal experience, as adherence in freedom to the present event of Christ.'[27]

In September 2010, Chiara Luce Badano from the Focolare Movement was beatified. She was a young Italian teenager who died of a painful bone cancer in 1990. It is hoped that she will be the first of many modern saints coming from the new movements, which the Pope now sees as producing 'witnesses of holiness'.

## My Own Voyage of Discovery Among Movements in Ireland

When I came up with the idea of writing a series of articles about the new ecclesial movements, I had no idea of the adventure that awaited me. I was involved myself in one movement, and remembered with great fondness when, a year after Pope John Paul II's historic meeting

27. Address of Pope Benedict XVI to the Bishops at the Shrine of Our Lady in Fatima, 13 May 2010.

with the movements in St Peter's Square, we had all come together for the first time in UCD. It was Pentecost 1999. We had heard of each others' names and perhaps had some ideas about some well-established groups like the Legion of Mary, but for many of us, the other groups were completely unknown.

Lots of the groups had their own music. We decided to put together a music group and learn each others' songs and we used to meet in my house. For months beforehand a group of us from Charismatic Renewal, Cell System of Evangelisation, Focolare and CL met regularly to learn the 'new' songs and practise together. Each group had a different singing style – from the formal choral style (with many harmonies and a conductor) of CL, to the 'see where the Spirit takes us' style of Charismatic Renewal. Working together forged a friendship and unity between us that remains to this day.

The meeting in UCD on 23 May 1999, which drew together 1,200 people from around twenty movements, was a resounding success. As each group shared the story of their charism and described their work, the over-riding impression was one of tremendous joy and gratitude. We were all part of the great mosaic of the Church. Each group had its own style (clear from the different styles of music), form of apostolate and ministry, but somehow we all completed each other. There was a remarkable and beautiful synergy in the Church, fruit of the Holy Spirit, with all of these groups working in different areas to bring about Christ's plan of salvation for the world.

Fast forward twelve years. I was working as a freelance journalist and, casting about for ideas, I thought of a series on the new movements and pitched the idea to a few magazines. Father Gerard Maloney, editor at *Reality* immediately said yes and the adventure began.

My idea was to visit each group, experience a typical gathering and write of the effects the spirituality of that group had on its members. Each month I became an honorary member of one or another group, including Legion of Mary, Youth 2000, L'Arche, Focolare, Catholic Charismatic Renewal, the Community of Nazareth, Communion and Liberation, Teams of Our Lady, Cells System of Evangelisation and Cursillo. It was a fantastic experience. While around me scandals over child abuse continued to outrage the public and people in the pews became more and more disheartened, here I found a vibrant, alive Catholic Church full of people who were excited by their faith, who had a real experience of Christian life and to whom traditional Catholic teachings made perfect sense because they were living as part of a Christian community.

Each group was different. I experienced the service of the local Church in all its needs in the Legion of Mary; the outreach to lukewarm Christians or those without faith in Cursillo; the intellectual stimulation of faith-filled reason in Communion and Liberation; the dynamism of a modern spirituality that impacts economy, politics and culture in Focolare; the great humanity of valuing all life in L'Arche; the transformation of parishes into living Christian communities in the Cells System of Evangelisation; the power of faith in the Charismatics; the translation into life of Catholic teaching on marriage in the Teams of Our Lady; the ability to pass on a vibrant Christian faith in families from generation to generation in the Community of Nazareth; and the evangelising enthusiasm of youth in Youth 2000.

I hope this 'walk' through ten of the new movements will be for each reader an impetus to faith and love, and a realisation that, as St Bernard of Clairvaux wrote, 'we all need each other' to bring about God's plan for a civilisation of love. To quote the twelfth-century saint, writing of his and other religious groups of the time:

> I admire them all. I belong to one of them by observance, but to all of them by charity. We all need one another: the spiritual good which I do not own and possess, I receive from others ... In this exile, the Church is still on pilgrimage and is, in a certain sense, plural: she is a single plurality and a plural unity. All our diversities, which make manifest the richness of God's gifts, will continue to exist in the one house of the Father, which has many rooms. Now there is a division of graces; then there will be distinction of glory. Unity, both here and there, consists in one and the same charity.[28]

---

28. Cf. St Bernard of Clairvaux, Apologia to William of St Thierry 4.8, cited in John Paul II, Apostolic Exhortation, *Vita Consecrata*, n. 52.

# ⥸1⥸
# The Legion of Mary

WE SAT IN THE SACRISTY, A SMALL GROUP OF WOMEN. One lady laid out the 'Legion of Mary' embroidered cloth on the table and placed flowers, a statue of Our Lady and the Legion standard on it. Another distributed the books. I was handed a copy of the prayers and the handbook. This was the 1220th meeting of this Praesidium in Prosperous, Co. Kildare, and my first.

I recognised the women. They are the backbone of my parish. You can ask them for help with anything and they will always say yes. Some I associated with the Legion of Mary, others I didn't, but I wasn't surprised to see them there.

I say it was my first meeting, but then I realise it was not. Years ago, as a schoolgirl, I was invited to a Legion meeting and went. But as soon as they began to call me 'Sister Susan', I panicked, thinking it was a channel to the convent.

'We use the words Sister and Brother because in the handbook we are a fraternity,' Betty O'Connor, who led the Prosperous meeting that day, told me. 'It gives us a closeness.' It makes sense.

There are an estimated four million members of the Legion of Mary (3,000 of them in Ireland), scattered across 170 countries, on five continents. They have another ten million auxiliary members who are the prayer powerhouse of the organisation. 'It is their prayer that helps us in our active work,' says Mary Murphy, a member of the Concilium (Central Committee). 'Some are housebound and they spend the whole day in prayer.'

According to Betty O'Connor, there is a Legion meeting happening 'almost at every moment somewhere in the world.'

It has very strong links with Dublin where it started, has its headquarters, and where its beloved founder and Servant of God, Frank Duff, is buried. The Legion of Mary, dating back to 1921, is one of the oldest lay movements in the Church.

Frank Duff was the eldest of seven children, and followed his father into the civil service. Due to ill health, his father retired at forty-two, and Frank became the breadwinner for the whole family. He had a strong prayer life, but when he joined the Society of St Vincent de Paul at twenty-four, his faith escalated to a new level.

Suddenly he was exposed to the harsh reality of poverty. After a time, his concern for the materially poor became a concern for the spiritually malnourished. With a friend, he set up a Catholic soup kitchen to provide an alternative to Protestant soup kitchens of the time.

But inside, a more rudimentary thought was developing. It was the simple idea that everyone born was called to become a saint by doing their 'ordinary duties extraordinarily well', with the object of pleasing God.

In 1916, aged twenty-seven, he published his first booklet *Can We Be Saints?*, in which he proposed to fellow Catholics that they set out on the journey towards sanctity. 'I ... simply set my face to follow out unswervingly, untiringly, the common life which day by day stretches before me, satisfied if in it I love You, and try to make You loved.'[29] In it, he emphasises the elements that would become hallmarks of the Legion – prayer, the Mass, devotion to Our Lady and St Joseph,

29. Frank Duff, *Can We Be Saints?* (Dublin: Veritas, 1929; reprinted 1998, Legion of Mary, Dublin), p. 6.

the importance of spiritual reading and friendship. 'Look only for good qualities in anyone you meet; you will find them. Never look for faults, for you would find them. Act thus, and you will easily develop the habit of love.'[30]

At age thirty-two, Frank Duff founded the Legion of Mary. This is a lay apostolic organisation at the service of the Church, under ecclesiastical guidance. Its aim is for its members to become holy and to advance the reign of Christ through Our Lady.

It was perhaps his civil service training that instilled in Duff a strong sense of organisation. The Legion handbook, which he wrote, lays out a precise format for meetings which is followed all over the world. Local groups are linked to regional groups, which are linked to the headquarters and a democratically elected council. Meetings involve saying the Rosary and opening prayers and the Catena.[31] In Latin, *catena* means link or chain. Saying this prayer is the chain that binds together all members of the Legion.

After the Rosary is said, there is reading of the minutes of the last meeting, spiritual direction, a reading from the handbook and discussion of practical matters, like the visits members have made or will make to the sick. Everything that happens at the meeting is recorded but confidential. There is great transparency. The handbook speaks of the duty of members to furnish 'audible' reports of their work. The Legion, to my knowledge, is and has been scandal-free, and it is perhaps this great transparency that has ensured this. They also have to

---

30. Ibid., p. 43.

31. The Catena begins and ends with an antiphon: 'Who is she that comes forth as the morning rising, fair as the moon, bright as the sun, terrible as an army set in battle array?' In between the two antiphons is Our Lady's *Magnificat* (cf. Lk 1:46-55).

perform 'substantial active legionary work'. In Prosperous they visit the sick and bereaved in their homes, as well as the sick in two local nursing homes. They also run the parish shop.

Betty joined the Junior Legion as a teenager. 'It made me more aware of my Christian faith and how you can be helping or sympathetic to other people and help them with your prayers, if nothing else.'

'You get things mysteriously,' said Josie Lawlor, another member. 'Our Lady sends them to you. If you are willing to give yourself to Our Lady, she distributes the graces after we pray.'

Long before the Second Vatican Council, Frank Duff saw the need to mobilise the laity as apostles. But for him it was not enough to convert people to the faith; you had to help them in practical ways. So it was that he, and the Legion following his example, came to found a great number of social works.

In 1922, while visiting a house in Dublin, Duff was appalled to discover that thirty women engaged in prostitution lived there. At the time he was working full time in the civil service. With a few priests he organised a retreat for the women, but realised they needed support and somewhere different to go afterwards. This was the beginning of the Sancta Maria hostel for 'friendless' girls.

In 1927 he set up the Morning Star for homeless men, and three years later, Regina Coeli, for homeless women and children. At that time there was no state institution where an unmarried mother could keep and continue to rear a child herself. Duff thought it was very wrong to break up a family. In 1948 he wrote that he believed the difficulties encountered by children when they left state institutions was attributable to 'the absence of the children's mothers during a period of life when such is necessary to the children. The consequence is that a peculiar and unnatural life is lived by those children.'[32]

The work in these two hostels has continued since the foundation of the Legion and is still continuing. Both hostels cater for around sixty to seventy people, though at the time of writing the Morning Star is being refurbished, and so caters for a smaller number. Both hostels operate with no state support and are staffed by Legion volunteers. (In the Legion, everyone works on a voluntary basis, as was recommended by Duff from the very start.)

In recent years, the Legion of Mary has been associated with a number of actions targeted at the sex industry. They were instrumental (together with local residents) in closing down a lap-dancing club in central Dublin in 2006, and often do street apostolate in Dublin city, praying outside sex shops and distributing leaflets and miraculous medals in streets associated with drug pushing.

Mary Murphy, from the central council (Concilium), is emphatic however that the Legion reaches out to everyone. They are not 'campaigning against' something (like pornography or prostitution), but rather they 'approach people' who happen to be working in these areas (even drug pushers). 'Our apostolate is personal contact,' she says.

Most members of the Legion in Ireland have been with it a long time, but in recent years the association has begun to attract the young again. Recent conferences of the Junior Legion have been attended by hundreds of young people. 'There was always a trickle, but it has improved recently,' Ann Murray from the central council told me.

---

32. Finola Kennedy, *Frank Duff: A Life Story* (London: Continuum, 2011), p. 93.

In other countries, like Brazil, there is a younger, more vibrant reality. Tadhg McMahon was one of those who brought the Legion there fifty years ago. He spent three years, in his own words, 'traipsing around the place, even on horseback', helping to set it up. Today he is the link person with Brazil, which now has over 400,000 active members. A former RE teacher, the Legion has given him a new understanding of the Church. 'The Legion raises the laity and raises the function of the priest', he says.

From Ireland, the Legion still sends groups to the UK and mainland Europe where they go door to door inviting Catholics to become involved in the Legion and local parish, and non-Catholics to consider joining the Catholic Church. This *Peregrinatio pro Christo* (Pilgrimage for Christ) lasts a week, and a fourteen-strong team can call to as many as nine hundred houses. 'It is an absolutely wonderful experience', says Ann Murray. 'You meet so many people. The Lord and his Mother are operating in a special way.'

Frank Duff died in 1980 and was buried in Glasnevin cemetery. Sixteen years later, the Archbishop of Dublin, Dr Desmond Connell, opened the cause of his canonisation. The process is going well, says Tadgh McMahon. 'We get reports of "favours received" from all over the world.' A Brazilian man was shot six times, prayed to Frank Duff and recovered. 'But it's hard to prove a miracle.'

At a time when his Church is suffering so severely because of the lack of holiness of some of its members, Frank Duff's humble, yet extraordinary life is an eloquent testament to what he preached – everyone is called to be a saint and everyone is called to be an apostle.

Giving his last public address in October 1980, a month before his death, he was filled with optimism for the future of the Church and spoke of dreaming 'with Mary' of bringing the whole world to her Son. He recalled a meeting a month earlier when he and other Legion leaders had spent a day plotting strategy as they poured over maps. How could they bring the Faith 'to three thousand five hundred million people who have not got it; while at the same time stirring up the five hundred million who have the Faith but who should have it better?'

According to biographer Finola Kennedy, 'Duff believed that the Legion provided the way to tackle the task. He told Legionaries that "Dreaming with Mary is the most solid of actions for she adds in the substance." He urged them to "think in terms of the apparently impossible" and concluded, "Mary will make the dream come true."'[33]

---

33. Ibid., p. 237.

# =2=
# Bring a Friend to Christ: Cursillo

EDEL WAS AT A CROSSROADS IN HER LIFE. SHE WAS twenty-six, single, working as a waitress and trying to rear her two young sons. 'I was stuck. I didn't know what way to turn. People used to say "Smile!" I used to think "What's the point of smiling?."'

She had given up going to the sacraments, but as she watched her grandmother dying a year ago, she admired the witness of her great faith. Edel had heard of Cursillo and decided she would go on one of their weekends.

'It was the best experience of my life,' she tells me, just weeks after her first Cursillo weekend. She is now going to Mass regularly, and each night she lights a candle and says the Rosary with her eight-year-old son Jake, who is preparing for First Communion. 'He loves it. He says "Go Mommy, say those prayers and stuff,"' she tells me in her Derry accent.

Before the Cursillo retreat Edel worried a lot about her future. Now she has handed her worries over to God. 'I wasn't eating or sleeping and now I'd sleep around the clock, so it has changed my life for the better.'

Connie Martin has been in Cursillo for twenty-five years. 'Cursillo brings people back to God,' he tells me. A former president of the group in Derry, he has seen many 'miracles'. 'People are visibly changed at the end [of the weekend]. It is the Holy Spirit.'

Like many in Cursillo, he had lapsed from his faith doing only 'wakes, funerals and weddings'. Yet on the

Monday after his Cursillo weekend, he was at evening Mass. 'People saw me and thought "there must be something wrong in the house".' But soon they noticed it was a regular occurrence.

Cursillo was founded in Majorca, Spain, by a group of laymen in 1944, including Eduardo Bonnin – the person most associated with its birth. Eduardo came from a devout Catholic family, but his years in the army brought him into contact with another reality. He realised the lives of the soldiers were very different to the lives of his Catholic family and friends. After doing a course for Pilgrim Leaders organised by Catholic Action, Eduardo became fascinated by a new idea – to develop a Cursillo that would not just prepare for a pilgrimage to a Marian shrine, but prepare for the lifelong pilgrimage towards the Father. The course should be for people without any religious convictions, like his army friends, those 'far away' from the Church. He began to work on his thinking, which he outlined in a paper named 'The Study of the Environment'.

Eduardo shared his ideas with some of the young people from Catholic Action and they too became enthusiastic about this new method and together decided to put it into practice. In 1944 the first Cursillo, devised by Bonnin and his friends, was held in Cala Figuera for fourteen men aged between thirteen and twenty-eight years. They adapted the earlier Cursillo, being used by Catholic Action for people without faith, and shortened the length of the retreat. Such was the success of this and subsequent courses (aimed at bringing young people back to the faith) that they spread rapidly with communities growing up around them.

Today the movement is present in sixty-five countries and a staggering eight million people have done the

Cursillo course. In Ireland, Cursillo is in Dublin, Cork, Dundalk, Donegal, Roscommon, Belfast, Newry and Derry. Around 2,000 people have done the course in Derry alone since it began in 1985.

Eduardo Bonnin died in February 2008, aged ninety. Except for nine years of military service, he worked in the family almond business on Majorca. He never married and spent his holidays giving Cursillo retreats, and his weeknights visiting prisoners and befriending others.

After his death, Bob Robinson, from Cursillo in Canada, spoke of Bonnin's concern for others: of the prisoner he visited for twenty years, but never tried to convert, of the two hardened murderers he visited the night before their executions, who went peacefully to their deaths because they had believed Bonnin's conversation-starter: 'You are very lucky. You will see Christ tomorrow.'

Bonnin always believed that the aim of the 'Cursillo in Christianity' was to give people the good news that God loved them, and that this had to be communicated through friendship. 'You can't say to someone, "You must go to Church." You say, "You must be a friend of mine." When the bridge is built, then you can speak of Christ,' he said.

The Cursillo he developed back in 1944 became the basis of the Cursillos that have run ever since, which focus on showing lay people how to become effective leaders over the course of a three-day weekend retreat. The emphasis of the weekend is to ask participants to take what they have learned back into the world, on what they call the 'fourth day'.

'The fourth day is the rest of your life,' says Seán, a former fitter, who was a 'chronic alcoholic'. At twenty-one he married Patricia and they had three children, but his drinking never let up. When he was thirty-five

Seán did the course. 'It was like an explosion of love. I was introduced to the God of love.' But even with his discovery, he was gripped by his addiction, reaching despair and attempting suicide. His wife put him out of the house, and aged thirty-nine, five years after his meeting with Christ, Seán was in hospital. 'One night I was out of my head, shaking and vomiting and I knelt down and said "Jesus, don't let me hurt anyone." I got up the way I am today,' he tells me.

His wife did not believe that he was finished with drink, but over a period of time, helped too by medication, Seán proved himself – coming to the house each day, making dinner and babysitting and then leaving. After seven months, Patricia invited him home again and now they are both involved in running Cursillo in Derry. A younger son works with the teen branch. 'We've a great life today, God is good. I love helping people. I got my life from Christ,' Seán tells me.

In Derry they have two weekend retreats in March and two in November, and they are always single sex. If a woman is married, her husband must go first. This is to encourage men to get involved. The weekend is slightly shrouded in mystery. There are talks, Masses, confession, silence and lots of personal testimonies, but people will not tell you everything. 'You don't want to spoil it for other people,' Edel tells me.

Noel, a long-time member of Cursillo in Derry, gives me a basic rundown on the topics covered in the talks. The first looks at the participant's own ideals – what they aspired to when they were growing up. The second looks at the vocation of the layperson in the Church. The next three talks Noel describes as the basic 'tripod' of Cursillo spirituality: piety (looking at prayer and sacramental life), study, and action (which encourages participants to set an example, especially at home with the family). 'If others see your life improving, they want a bit of it,' says Noel. The sixth talk looks at leadership, and the seventh at Christian community in action (where they study the work of groups like the Society of St Vincent de Paul, the Legion of Mary and others). In the final talks, participants look at their own environment and what kind of an influence they do or can have in it, how they are going to live after the retreat and the importance of confidentiality.

Eight of the talks – based on guidelines that came originally from the founding group and were adapted in the US – are given by lay people. The leaders personalise the talks and share many of their own life stories. A priest gives another five talks about topics such as grace, the sacraments and obstacles to Christ and celebrates Mass each day.

'All the talks complement each other,' says Noel, 'and one flows naturally into another.'

May O'Donnell, from the Cursillo secretariat in Derry, tells me the story of how when her husband died suddenly some years ago, she passed through a real period of forsakenness. She sometimes shares this experience at Cursillo weekends. 'People realise they're not on their own. It can be emotional, but it can be very helpful,' she says.

In March 2012, thirty-four women and twenty-six men came to the two Cursillo retreats while another fifty people worked behind the scenes for both – praying, preparing talks, meals, music and accommodation.

Ciarán, age thirty-seven, was at the men's weekend. 'I learnt not to be looking at God up in the sky, but in the people around me, to interact with one another as if the other person is Christ.' He says the weekend was peaceful. 'I was able to put things to bed in my head.' He says he's 'still searching' but he's trying to change. Where he works as a mechanical engineer, it is a man's environment with a lot of coarse talk. After the Cursillo weekend, he found himself regretting taking part in some conversations. 'The way I look at things is different now. I want to be different.'

After the weekend, participants are invited to a weekly 'Friendship Night' and to form a small group where they can meet regularly, share how they're getting on and say the Rosary. In Derry, the 'Friendship Night' happens each Wednesday. They have a coffee bar which opens at 7.30 p.m., and for the first half hour or so people sit around chatting, catching up and making friends with people from other Cursillo courses. At 8.15 p.m. the whole group gathers before the Blessed Sacrament to say the Rosary, sing and pray.

People like Ciarán and Edel, who want to stay involved in the activities, can elect after a while to become part of a smaller sharing group. At these groups, the members meet on a regular basis, sharing their spiritual and day-to-day experiences, praying and supporting each other.

Noel has been meeting with his small group for nineteen years. 'You get to know each other very well. You pray and you really share each others' lives. You know if someone is sick.' At these smaller groups, the members try to monitor their own spiritual lives to see, for example, if they are managing to stick to practical proposals they have made for themselves, like to say the Rosary each day or to go to Mass more often.

The biggest event of the year for the group is the Walk to Knock in July. Groups from Belfast, Derry and Dublin converge on the shrine and walk around the Basilica together. Around 160 people went on the Derry walk in 2012 – a huge logistical challenge. Each day a lorry brought their camp beds, luggage and food ahead to the next stopover at a church or school hall. Other vehicles accompanied the walkers and provided water and respite. The walk involves people of all ages, including lots of young people (Search) and younger teenagers who belong to Cor (Christ in Others Retreat).

Bethany, sixteen, has been in Cor for two years. 'It is really enjoyable. You learn about yourself and you get to know God more.' She told no one about her first Cor retreat, but afterwards wanted to invite all her friends. Now she gets more out of Mass and is happy to support the Church's teachings on issues like sexual morality.

The two Cor retreats have strengthened her faith. 'It teaches you to respect other people. When you see what Jesus did in your life, you want to do it for him.'

# ≡3≡

# Finding God in Reality: Communion and Liberation

IT IS A CHILLY FRIDAY WINTER'S NIGHT. I WOULD like to be tucked up in front of a fire watching TV and sipping a glass of wine, but instead I find myself in Dublin, at a study session on the writings of Don Luigi Giussani, founder of Communion and Liberation. To my surprise about fifty others are here, aged from nineteen to late forties. Many are students. This is the School of Community, a weekly catechesis session that forms people in the spirituality of CL. This year they are studying Don Giusanni's first book, *The Religious Sense*.

The gathering starts with some beautiful singing, and then it is down to study. Last week they studied a passage which begins: 'Upon gazing at reality, I have before me something which produces openness ... I do not react to reality as a photographic film, upon which reality 'impresses' its image and that's that. Not only does reality make an impression on me, it also moves me and solicits me to engage in and search for some other thing, something beyond immediate appearances.'[34]

In silence they review the text, then people share how they have applied it to their everyday lives.

Martin, a doctor, tells of a training exercise earlier in the week. A presentation by a psychologist put forward a vision of the ideal life that did not correspond to his

---

34. Luigi Giussani, *The Religious Sense*, trans. John Zucchi (Montreal: McGill Queens University Press, 1997), p. 110.

experience as a Christian. She advised the group to annihilate their desires and in that way avoid suffering. Martin's experience was that desire was what defined people as humans; however, he was grateful for the training even if he disagreed with some of the core principles. 'I realised that everything can be used to open a dialogue with your colleagues,' he shares with the group.

Martha, a childminder, shares an experience of 'responding to reality' on her day off. She wondered what she would do, and then visitors came one by one to see her. 'It was very full. Applying this [responding to reality], I'm more alive than I've felt in a long time. My daughter was upset because she had lost a purse, but then she told me "Within five minutes of being with you, Mum, I'm happy again."'

Sergio, a young student, tells how he experiences 'signs' of God all the time. 'Every time I have a question, or I need to learn something, I am given the opportunity to acquire this knowledge. This is a sign that someone is looking after me, showing me the way.'

Mauro Biondi, who leads the weekly School of Community, explains that often Christians, when they leave home to face the world, see reality as an enemy. Instead, he emphasises, we are called to engage with reality.

To illustrate this, he shares a personal experience. He is manager of a language school and a while back he was at yet another travel fair. He's been to many, and was feeling a bit jaded. His new assistant was full of enthusiasm and 'seriousness'. He thought, 'This lady is better at this work than I am.' But what surprised and impressed him was that instead of fearing that she would be poached by a competitor (and take business with her), or feeling envious, his thought was one of gratitude. This attitude he discovered in himself was a sign of God's presence. Shortly after, he was speaking to a manager from another company who was saying how important it is to poach people with experience so as not to waste time training them and to get hold of their contacts. 'I said, "You're right,"' Mauro tells the students, 'but added my observations: "If you always employ people with experience, where will the young get experience? In addition you miss the chance to get to know someone and share your vision of the company with them."' His colleague answered, 'You're right!'

In CL, reason leads to faith. 'As John Paul II said, Jesus Christ reveals the human person to himself, therefore reason is essential,' Mauro tells me.

It is a beautiful way of looking at faith. At the end of my first School of Community, I am tired but energised as everyone, chatting noisily, gathers to sing 'Happy Birthday' to one of the members, before heading to the pub for a Friday night drink.

Marianna, a twenty-one-year-old Brazilian studying International Business and Spanish, says it is the friendship that has drawn her to and kept her in the movement. Sara, from Ireland, a first-year student in TCD, agrees. Her parents are both in CL, and she feels privileged to have been exposed to this 'friendship' from a young age. 'The friendship with people helped me discover my relationship with God,' she says.

Communion and Liberation began in 1954 when Fr Luigi Giussani established a Christian presence in a secondary school in Milan with a group called Gioventú Studentesca (GS) or Student Youth. The name Communion and Liberation appeared for the first time in 1969.

His artistic father, a carver and restorer of wood, spurred the young Luigi to always question and seek the reason for things.

At the age of eleven, Luigi entered the diocesan seminary of Milan, continuing and finally completing his secondary school studies at the theological school of Venegono, north of Milan.

He studied intensely and discovered a new gift within himself – the ability to combine the divine and the human, theology and culture. He read poems by the nineteenth-century Romantic poet Leopardi as an accompaniment to meditation after the Eucharist. The conviction grew in him that the peak of all human genius, no matter how or where it was expressed, was the prophecy of the coming of Christ.

So he recognised in Leopardi's poem '*Alla sua donna*' ('To his Woman') a kind of introduction to the prologue to John's Gospel; in Beethoven's music he saw the vivid expression of the eternal religious sense of man. For Giussani the human heart was a need for beauty, justice and truth that could only be filled by God.

After ordination in 1945 he lectured, but in 1954 he sought permission to leave his chair as Professor of Catholic Dogma and Oriental Theology at Milan's Major Ambrosian Seminary and take up a post as teacher of religion at a local college.

In one of his many books, Giussani tells of the episode that prompted his decision: 'During a holiday train trip to the Adriatic Sea, I started a conversation with some secondary school students and found them shockingly ignorant of the Church and Church teachings. I had to assume that their ignorance was caused by complete indifference toward, and in some cases even disgust with, the Church. At that point, I decided to devote my life to restoring a Christian presence at secondary school level.'[35]

Another incident had a profound effect on his mission. 'Not long after becoming a religion teacher at Berchet (a secondary school in Milan), I noticed a group of young people who always met on the stairs during the breaks between classes and spoke with great intensity and animation. Once I asked them what they were talking about, and they responded: "Communism." I wondered why Christianity was not capable of inspiring such fervour and unity among young people, something which Christ himself had desired ...

'One day, returning from work and ruminating on that incapacity of Christianity to inspire youth, I encountered four boys deep in discussion. I asked if they were Christians, and they answered "Yes," but a bit uneasily. Then I continued. "You say you are Christians, but in the school assemblies, only the Communists and Fascist-Monarchists debate together. Where are the Christians?" The next week these four started a debate in the school assembly, introducing themselves as "we Catholics". From that moment and for the next ten years, Christianity and the Church were the most heatedly debated topics in school meetings.'[36]

This was the start of Gioventú Studentesca (Student Youth). But in 1968, against the background of the student riots in Milan, GS went through a profound crisis when a number of its leaders became Marxists or anarchists. A year later, Communion and Liberation was born. The name was important. By including the word 'liberation', the students were declaring that liberation

35. Luigi Giussani and Robi Ronza, *Comunione e Liberazione* (Milan: Jaca Books, 1987), p. 21.

36. Ibid.

(happiness, justice, etc.) did not come from political revolution, but from communion with Christ. Through Giussani's educational method, people met Christ, the perfect man, and they discovered themselves and true happiness.

Don Giussani died in 2005. On the seventh anniversary of his death in February 2012, the first steps were taken towards his beatification when CL formally requested the Archbishop of Milan, Cardinal Angelo Scola, to open the process of investigation into his life, virtues and holiness. By then the movement was present in about seventy countries.

Communion and Liberation came to life quite naturally in Ireland, when an Italian member came to study in UCD in 1980. He could not forget the experience of CL he had lived in Italy and so brought it with him. Soon he was joined by other students. Mauro Biondi also came as a university student, met his Irish wife, Margaret, and they settled down to become the first stable presence of the movement here.

Today there are people associated with CL living in Dublin, Naas, Limerick and Cork. Most of its adherents go to the weekly School of Community. They are mainly lay Catholics, but CL involves priests and religious too, as well as consecrated laymen and women who are committed to lifelong celibacy, known as the Memores Domini. There is one such community in Dublin, made up of four men. Participation in CL can involve a relatively low degree of commitment, such as attending a weekly School of Community, or a high degree of commitment such as enrolling in the Fraternity of Communion and Liberation. Since 1982 this has been the part of the movement that has been given official Church recognition.

The movement spreads organically from friend to friend. For two years Owen Sorenson from Dublin had two friends involved in CL without knowing it. They used to tell him they were going to a meeting on Friday nights, while he went to the pub with other friends. 'After six months I was curious to find out what the meeting was,' he says. He went along to the School of Community. 'I found what was said at the meeting and in the book made sense and answered questions I had about faith. It was more useful and interesting than speaking about rubbish in the pub!' he adds, laughing.

Owen met his wife Raffi through CL. She is from Brescia in Italy and grew up in a family where there was no practice of faith. 'I wasn't happy. I was looking for something,' she says. When she was sixteen a friend invited her to a Mass. 'I remember the sermon. I felt as though the priest was talking to me.' Soon Raffi was involved with the young people and living a life of faith. The couple now have five children, some of whom are involved in the movement. The spirituality of CL has given them great light in their marriage. 'It has helped me to understand what Catholic marriage is and to live it,' says Raffi. 'By getting married you're saying yes to a vocation and you're together to help one another in that. I don't expect my ultimate happiness to come from Owen, but helping each other to go deeper into our faith makes me happy, and then he becomes indispensable to me – the most important person in my life.'

# 4

# Living Gospel Unity:
# Focolare

SALLY GREW UP IN BELFAST DURING THE TROUBLES.
On the brink of joining the terrorists 'because they
seemed the only ones ready to give their life for what they
believed in', she went to an international youth festival
organised by Focolare. She heard about a different choice
– the choice of Gospel love, and decided to live that way
instead.

Soon her choice was tested. Out buying milk one day,
she was beaten up by a gang of youths. 'As they slammed
a brick into the base of my spine, I thought, "If you
believe in what you heard – now is the time to put it into
practice. Forgiveness begins here."'

Another time, she was taken in for questioning by
British soldiers following a massive explosion. Terrified,
she asked herself: 'What would the people from the
Focolare say and do in a situation like this? They would
say, "The only thing that will remain of this moment is
how much you try to love." So, very tentatively, Sally
began to talk to the soldiers, asking them about their lives
and families. She realised they were as frightened as her.
After three hours they released her. 'I felt a tremendous
sense of peace inside as I walked home at about 3 a.m. I
had taken on board a lifestyle that I knew I couldn't go
back on,' she recounts.

Mary from Navan studied law in UCD. Interrupting
her studies, she went to London to try out religious
life for some months, but it didn't work out. Returning

disappointed to Ireland, one evening she went to a Word of Life meeting at the university. The young people shared how they tried to live out a sentence from the Gospel. Mary decided to try it out. She was shy by nature, but when she got on the bus that evening, she noticed an old beggar woman sitting alone. She sat beside her and began to talk to her. As she went to leave the bus, the woman spoke. 'Thanks for talking to me. Not many people do that these days.' Mary experienced a new happiness. She realised she didn't have to join a religious order to follow God. She could live the Gospel where she was in every moment.

These are just two of the hundreds of stories of people in Ireland whose lives have been transformed through living the Gospel-based spirituality of Focolare, which came to life during the Second World War and reached Ireland forty years ago.

Against the backdrop of the war, in Trent, northern Italy, its founder Chiara Lubich and a group of girls (aged fifteen to twenty-three) unleashed their own revolution. Each night they fled to the air-raid shelter and brought a copy of the Gospels with them. They read from it and started to systematically live out its words.

One week, for example, they were living 'Give and there will be gifts for you.' A poor man came to their little flat looking for food. They gave him the only food they had, an apple. Shortly after, someone brought them a gift – a bag of apples. They gave these away too. That evening a friend arrived from the country with sacks of apples. They called it the apple day. The Gospel and its promises were verified before their eyes.

'Jesus had made a promise and he was keeping it,' wrote Lubich. 'So the Gospel was credible, it was true. We shared with everyone what was happening each day and they were amazed. Many were struck by the truth of the Gospel; they wanted to experience the same thing and follow Jesus. These astonishing new experiences of the Gospel circulated from mouth to mouth. They were a small echo of the words of the apostles: Christ is risen. Now it was: Christ is alive!'[37]

Young people and adults from different backgrounds were attracted by this radical Gospel-based lifestyle and joined that first group of girls. Soon families, people of every social status and age group as well as priests and people in religious life, formed part of the growing community.

Chiara and her companions in the first Focolare shared not only spiritual goods (their experiences of Gospel life), but also material goods, following the example of the first Christians.[38] The wider community shared the extra they had or their needs, and those who could committed themselves to giving a monthly sum. With the money received, they tried to support families in need in the community. 'This was our aim: to reach the point where there would be no more people in need, and that everyone would have enough to live on,' wrote Lubich.[39]

After about six months, five hundred people in Trent were trying to live this Gospel-based spirituality. The bishop of Trent, Carlo De Ferrari, recognising it as a work of God, stated, 'There is God's finger here' and gave his first approval.

They were nicknamed *focolarini*, meaning 'people of fire', and their little flat became known as the *focolare* (or

---

37. Chiara Lubich, *Essential Writings* (London: New City Press, 2007), p. 6, from an address at Council Chambers of Bologna, 22 September 1997.

38. Acts 4:32, 34-35.

39. Chiara Lubich, 'Erano un cuor solo e un anima sola', *Amico Serafico* (1948), pp. 236-7.

hearth). Because there, even in the midst of the appalling destruction of the war, there was a joy, a light. It was the presence promised by Jesus when he said, 'Where two or more are gathered in my name, I am there in their midst' (Mt 18:20).

One night they sheltered from the bombs in a cellar and by candlelight read Jesus' last testament: 'Father, may they all be one.' Chiara said it was as if the words were lit up from underneath and they had an intuition that this was their mission in life – to contribute towards bringing about the fulfilment of those words. They asked Jesus in the Eucharist to make them instruments of unity in the world.

And this is what happened. Over the following fifty-five years (until Chiara Lubich died in 2008), the movement spread geographically to 186 countries, and within all the Christian churches, and indeed the great Oriental religions. Today about 150,000 are closely associated with it, and millions in contact – Christians, Jews, Muslims, Hindus, Sikhs and Buddhists.

Our unity with non-Christians is based around the belief that we are all brothers and sisters, children of the one Father, says Juanita Majury, co-director of Focolare in Ireland. 'Instead of looking at our differences, we try to emphasise and to live the Golden Rule – "Treat everyone as you would like to be treated yourself", which is common to all the great religions. It is our experience, for example with our Sikh friends here in Ireland, that this creates a great current of love between us which unites us beyond all our differences.'

The movement arrived in Ireland in 1972, and today has five Focolare centres – two in Dublin, two in Kildare and one in Belfast. Here core members who have consecrated their lives to God (*focolarini*) try to live the way Chiara and her first companions did in the first Focolare centre in Trent, and always have the presence of Jesus in their midst. There are also communities of the Focolare in places where there are no centres, like Limerick, Cork, Cavan, Antrim, Rostrevor, Monaghan, Dungarvan and Kilkenny.

'I think it has brought a huge light among families,' comments David Hickey, co-director of Focolare in Ireland. 'It has spread among and through families, to their children as well, and in this way it has become present all over Ireland in a very natural way.'

I went to a family afternoon at the Focolare centre in Kildare. The former hotel was teeming with life and children. Families from Dublin, Limerick, Kildare and Meath ate lunch together, and then we split for separate programmes. With the adults we had a session on communication in the family, starting with a Gospel-based meditation and followed by moving personal stories about the art of communication, which brings the presence of Jesus into the family. With his presence we learnt that even the most painful family situations could be faced and resolved.

Downstairs the young children played a game centred on the Cube of Love – a dice displaying six mottos on Jesus' art of loving. The family rolls the cube each morning, and tries to live the phrase which comes up, like 'Love your neighbour' or 'Be the first to love.'[40] Afterwards, they tell each other how they got on. 'My mum asked me to make my bed,' shared Katie, aged seven. I didn't want to but I did it anyway. I was the first to love.' In other rooms, teenagers had workshops on music, sport and dance in preparation for the International Eucharistic Congress.

---

40. The Cube of Love is also used in some schools.

Over the years, Focolare has also attracted people who are trying to bring Gospel values into business. Many of these have been drawn to the Economy of Communion (EOC), a new economic paradigm where the profits of the business are split, with a portion going to help economic initiatives in the most disadvantaged parts of the world. There are about 800 EOC businesses worldwide.

What is new about the Economy of Communion, Mullingar company director Donal Lawlor told me, is the way it puts the emphasis on 'communion' – living in communion in the business. 'That is not just a sharing of money but the way decisions are made and the whole sharing within the business.' There are EOC businesses in Dublin, Kildare and Cavan.

In 1998 the Focolare purchased a small family-run hotel (the venue for the family afternoon), where they built three houses and a cottage. A number of families moved to the nearby village of Prosperous. 'We want to be a focal point for the movement in Ireland,' says David Hickey, 'so people can come and be rejuvenated by the presence of Jesus in our midst.' The centre is used not just by the movement, but also by other church movements and local businesses, who often remark on its strong 'spiritual atmosphere'.

One of the houses is for priests. Father Hugh Kavanagh, parish priest in a working-class area of west Dublin, says sharing his life with other priests inspires and encourages him, and he has understood priesthood as a Marian priesthood. 'My ministry, as a priest, of celebrating Mass and the sacraments is very important for the Christian community. But I am called to live my priesthood, in the same way as Mary worked silently in the background, in the service of others. It's a service that reaches out and builds communion with everyone – priests, parishioners and with the bishop.'

Father Kavanagh sees a face of Jesus on the cross in the current dark moment for the Church. 'This collapse of everything gives me a new understanding of him. When he cried out "Why?" he experienced total failure, the apparent collapse of his mission. Embracing this experience makes me believe that we can contribute to a new dawn, a new resurrection, a new life for the Church in Ireland.'

The gift Focolare gives to the Church is the charism of unity. According to Chiara Lubich, for two people to become one it is necessary for each to die to their own desires and feelings so that they are completely present to the other person. Doing this, each is enriched by the virtue of the other person, each becomes the other. Living unity in this way mirrors the life of the Trinity, she says. 'Whoever lives unity, lives Jesus and lives the Father. He or she lives in heaven, in paradise always: the earthly here, made paradise through the hundredfold, and the heavenly on high, through life eternal.'[41]

---

41. Chiara Lubich, *Essential Writings*, p. 109.

# 5

# Living Beatitudes:
# The L'Arche Community

GINA WORKS PART-TIME IN A CAFÉ. NORA WALKS TO work each day and cooks her own dinner in the evening. Declan is taking his driving simulation test, while Frances booked an appointment to have her hair done today on her own.

A big deal? Yes, because each of these people has an intellectual disability. Each task is an achievement. Gina, Nora, Declan and Frances are part of L'Arche, a community where people with and without intellectual disabilities live together.

'People with intellectual disabilities were hidden, and still today they can be hidden. But they contribute incredible value to your life. They give you the insight to see what is important in life,' Gretta McIlvern told me as we walked around L'Arche community centre in Callan, Co. Kilkenny.

Gretta, a former nurse with the National Health Service in Northern Ireland, is community leader of the fifty-five-strong L'Arche community in Callan, which includes twenty-four 'core members' (people with disabilities), and fourteen voluntary assistants who live for a period in the community.

'Everything you encounter or experience in your life leads to today, that is the path of life,' she tells me. They are words that could have been spoken by the founder of L'Arche, Jean Vanier. This charismatic man, now in his eighties, founded L'Arche in 1964. Son of a former

Governor General of Canada, Jean spent his childhood in England until the outbreak of World War II, when he and his four brothers and one sister were sent back to Canada.

He joined the Royal Navy, becoming an officer in 1945. Despite the promising career that lay in front of him, Jean was more and more drawn to prayer and reflection on what God's call for him might be. In 1950, he resigned from the navy and went to study philosophy and theology at the Institut Catholique in Paris. There he met Fr Thomas Philippe, a Dominican priest and professor who became his spiritual mentor and friend.

In 1963, having published his doctoral thesis on Aristotle, Vanier returned to Canada to teach at the University of Toronto, but within a short time went back to France to visit his friend who was working as chaplain to a small residence for people with special needs. The visit was a turning point in his life. He realised God was calling him to something new. He decided to stay, and in 1964 invited two of the men from the institution to live with him.

Years later, describing the experience, he said that living with Raphael and Philippe helped him discover himself and was a great joy. 'I began to find the child in myself. I was never so happy as when I was living with them in a very simple way in a little house, working together, having fun together, praying together. That is to say, I sensed a completely new meaning to my life, very different from when I was in the navy, very different from when I was teaching philosophy, but something much more fulfilling. It was a place where it was quite clear that Jesus was present.'[42]

---

42. From an interview with Jean Vanier on *30 Good Minutes* on WTTW 11 (PBS) in Chicago, aired 27 February 2000.

He named his house 'L'Arche,' the French word for Noah's Ark. In time, others joined them, until the community grew to over four hundred people.

'When you start living with people with disabilities, you begin to discover a whole lot of things about yourself,' says Vanier.[43] He learned that 'to be human is to be bonded together, each with our own weaknesses and strengths, because we need each other.'[44]

Spurred on by the example of this humble and inspiring man, other communities were born all over the world in the 1970s. (Now there are 139 communities.) Jean Vanier was invited to speak everywhere. His words and being radiated a gentle holiness.

'Every child, every person needs to know that they are a source of joy; every child, every person, needs to be celebrated. Only when all of our weaknesses are accepted as part of our humanity can our negative, broken self-images be transformed,' he said.

His message that everyone is of unique and sacred value resonated. His practical witness of communities of people with and without intellectual disabilities living together in love was convincing.

In 1975, a small group of people from the village of Kilmoganny, Co. Kilkenny (population 150 at the time) approached the Bishop of Ossory, Dr Peter Birch. They were concerned about the fate of Helen, a girl with special needs from the village. Her parents were worried about what would happen as they got older, if they were not able to care for her. Bishop Birch thought of his friend Jean Vanier and soon the wheels were in motion. A local publican donated a house and some land. By 1978,

---

43. Ibid.

44. *Maclean's* magazine, 4 September 2000, p. 33.

with huge local involvement, the house was ready and the first L'Arche community was born, consisting of two core members and a helper. Jean Vanier performed the opening. Having an Irish grandmother (a Moloney from Clare), Jean always had a soft spot for Ireland.

Over the years, other communities were established in Ireland – in Belfast, Dublin, Cork and Sligo, as well as a second community in Kilkenny. Each one is twinned with a L'Arche community in the developing world.

Nora is one of original core members in Callan. She tells me she is thirty-three, but then Gretta reminds her she's sixty! 'I understand,' I tell her. 'I only feel thirty-three too!' Recently Nora moved into a cottage of her own. 'I like it,' she tells me. Each day she walks the short distance from her home to the workshop where she weaves and knits. She buys food in the local supermarket and cooks her own dinner. With a huge smile on her face, she shows me how she weaves and introduces me to her friend Marie on the other loom.

While Nora lives alone, other core members live in communal residence on the same campus with voluntary assistants. There is a one-to-one ratio, with the core members always having a friend close at hand to help. During the day they attend workshops on things like candle-making, pottery, woodwork, photography, cookery and horticulture. Friends with intellectual disabilities join them at the workshops and return home to their families in the evening. For the core members, however, the modern, spacious residence where they eat and sleep at nighttime is home.

Hanna, twenty-five, an assistant from Ohio, lives in a house with four core members and three other helpers. On a typical day she'll help with meals, housekeeping, and assist three core members who live alone. She has one day off a week, and one long weekend a month. Hanna studied anthropology and came here for a year, but although far from home and only earning pocket money, she is happy and wants to stay longer. 'It is a really good experience,' she tells me.

Community life revolves around prayer and celebratory meals. The community is very much part of the life of the local parish and village, with core members involved at all levels. 'Nothing about us, without us,' Gretta quotes to me. 'When people are allowed and enabled to do what they're capable of, that gives them increased self-worth.' Showing the true value of people with disabilities is a freeing experience, not just for the children but for their parents too.

'Parents often have the feeling that they have to compensate for something, which may even be their own guilt at bringing a child with a disability into the world. Consequently they [the children] are seen as people who have to be cared for and have things done for them. I think if the world puts a better value on people with disabilities, parents do not have to feel guilty, but can help their child achieve his or her maximum potential at an early age,' says Gretta.

Love stories begin in L'Arche. One year there were five weddings among the L'Arche Kilkenny members. Peter and Mairead's story illustrates how this happens. They both arrived in the community in the late 1980s, intending to stay a year or two. They fell in love, married, had children and are now deeply imbedded, together with their two children, in the life of the Kilkenny community. 'There is a very good rapport between the family and our L'Arche life. It doesn't clash,' says Peter.

Before coming to L'Arche, Peter worked as a teacher. Now he is Assistants Coordinator at Callan, which involves a variety of people – from local Transition Year students, Fás and Maynooth seminarians – in short-term placements, which give them the opportunity to interact with the core members and be part of a L'Arche community.

Mairead sees the effect living in such close proximity to the core members has on their two teenage children. They have gained 'a rounded view of life and will talk to anybody, whether they have or haven't disabilities. They have learnt the value of people regardless of their IQ or position in society,' she says.

Since 2005, Mairead has been running Café L'Arche on Green Street in Callan – the first L'Arche-run café in the movement's history. Core members and staff work side by side in the kitchen of the quietly trendy eatery. Mairead plans to start a certified training course for the core members in the future.

The workshops (supported financially by the HSE and fundraising), four residential houses, independent living houses and café are impressive – a rich harvest. But according to Gretta, the real harvest is in the people with intellectual disabilities. This is true of the core members of all the L'Arche communities, no matter where they are.

Thomas is one of the core members in L'Arche Belfast, which celebrated its tenth anniversary in 2011. Every Monday morning at 7 a.m., he joins a cross-denominational prayer group in North Belfast and together they pray for an hour. In the beginning he found it hard to express himself and someone had to help him. But now he can do it on his own. 'I get up early. Nice time. Peace and quiet,' he says.

'He has a real passion for meeting people and for prayer,' Scott Shively, the leader of the community, tells me. 'Having Thomas with them at the group has really changed them. Now there are fewer discussions on big theological issues, and more on real issues.'

In Belfast, the community runs a catering service called Root Soup, as well as a garden project. Root Soup works in partnership with a temporary accommodation hostel (run by Open Door Housing Association) for unemployed or homeless young men and women who work side by side with the people with disabilities to provide the service.

The people with disabilities who go to the L'Arche workshops gain enormously from the experience. Michelle goes to the Callan workshop but lives at home. According to her mother, Ann, her speech, communication skills and cooking have all developed. 'She's into photography in a big way and learning to play the guitar. It's brilliant,' says Ann.

And the gain is not just in the core members, but in all. 'The friendship with the core members is amazing. Your life is changed. I never realised the truth of this until a year ago when my son said "Oh Mum, you've changed so much,"' remarks Gretta.

As Jean Vanier wrote: 'Communion is mutual trust, mutual belonging; it is the to-and-fro movement of love between two people where each one gives and each one receives. Communion is not a fixed state; it is an ever-growing and deepening reality that can turn sour if one person tries to possess the other, thus preventing growth. Community is mutual vulnerability and openness one to the other. It is liberation for both, indeed, where both are allowed to be themselves, where both are called to grow in greater freedom and openness to others and to the universe.'[45]

---

45. Jean Vanier, *Becoming Human* (New Jersey: Paulist Press, 1998), p. 28.

# ⹀6⹀
# Living Evangelisation: Parish Cells

BERNARD IS A MEMBER OF THE TRAVELLING community. He grew up in a society of 'violence and feuds'. For years he lived in Manchester and then came back to Ireland, living in halting sites around Dublin. Ten years ago he settled in Blanchardstown. A man he worked with invited him to his home one evening for a special gathering. That night Bernard went to his first 'cell' meeting at the home of Thomas and Bridie Clancy in Leixlip.

'My mother was very religious, but I had turned away from God,' Bernard tells me.

A warm welcome greeted him when he went into the Clancy home. He quietly joined around ten other people sitting in a circle around a candle in the kitchen. They sang, read from Scripture, gave thanks and shared personal experiences of how they had tried to share their faith with the people around them. Then in silence they listened to a short lesson on the Scripture they had already read, before spontaneously praying for their own needs, the needs of the parish and the world. At the end, holding hands and facing outwards, they said the Our Father.

'It wasn't like church. When you go to church, it is a community thing, but then people don't talk to each other. You go outside the door, and you leave each other,' recalls Bernard.

This was totally different. He felt at home, connected with people.

Since then Bernard has been a regular attendee of the cell meeting in Leixlip. The meetings take away his tension. 'Day-to-day living is very stressful. The cell releases that stress off of you,' he says.

It has given him a new vision of the Church. 'It is like [taking over] government – we are the Church. Faith comes from the heart.'

And when you leave, does it affect your daily life? I ask him. 'Of course! I try to live better, a more godly life. The prayer helps you a lot.'

Bernard was so taken with the cell meeting, that he immediately began to invite members of his family along. He was thankful to Thomas for inviting him, and wanted to extend the gift to others. A number came and left, but his seventeen-year-old daughter, Lisa, remained.

'I think it is lovely. When I leave, I'm not the same person as I was when I went in, because I feel a lot freer,' she tells me.

The Parish Cell System of Evangelisation aims at re-evangelising Catholic parishes. It is geared not just towards giving those present a real experience of faith, but also to encouraging them to evangelise the people they are in touch with in daily life.

It was started by an Irish-born priest, Monsignor Michael Eivers from Longford, who worked as parish priest in Florida. In the 1980s when he became ill, partly due to overwork, he pondered how he could lead his parish in ongoing spiritual growth, and not just be a weekly 'spiritual filling station.'

Father Eivers had a gut feeling that the answer lay in small groups. Hearing of the extraordinary success of small parish cell groups in a Pentecostal Church in Korea, Fr Eivers travelled to take part in a seminar lead by its pastor, Rev. David Cho. Father Eivers then applied his methodology and structure to his own Catholic parish.

He found that once he had provided initial training and built in ongoing supervision the groups took off, and his sense of responsibility for the parish decreased, as did his workload. Now he was surrounded by many co-workers. Within a few years, 550 parishioners were involved in dozens of cell groups in his parish. 'Of all the initiatives I have undertaken, cell groups yield the best fruit,' he said.[46]

News of Fr Eivers' success story spread. In February 1987, an Italian priest, Fr Pigi Perini, visited Fr Eivers' parish in Miami accompanied by ten parishioners so they could learn from this experience. Inspired by what they saw, they brought the system back to their own parish in Milan. After some years they had more than 1,100 people involved in cell groups in St Eustorgio parish.

Today there are parish cell groups in North and South America, Italy, Malta, France, the UK, Germany and Ireland, involving many thousands of people. In 2009 the Pontifical Council for the Laity recognised its international organisation and temporarily approved its statutes.

The movement came to Ireland in 1990 through Fr Michael Hurley, author of *Transforming Your Parish*. He was parish priest in the burgeoning suburb of Ballinteer in south County Dublin and was concerned about the widening gap he saw between faith and culture in people's lives. He had always been connected to groups that tried to bring people together in a prayer context, but it seemed to be impossible to draw more than forty people to a prayer activity in a parish.

---

46. See http://leixlipparishcells.com/history.html.

In 1989 he went to a retreat in Rome, where Fr Pigi
Perini spoke of his own experience of the cell system of
evangelisation. Through Fr Perini's broken English and
his own broken Italian, Fr Hurley understood enough
to think, 'This is something I'm going after.' Finally he
thought he had found a system to breach the faith–
culture gap, and to break through the 'forty people'
barrier. 'Potentially it involved hundreds of people in
transforming a parish,' he told me.

Arriving back from the Rome meeting, Fr Hurley
gathered a small group together from his parish of
Ballinteer, and then arranged for four of them, two young
married women, a young married man and himself, to
attend the first cell seminar in Milan. They were very
impressed by it. 'Our impression was that this was
something of the spirit of God and we wanted to take it
back to our parish,' he said.

For months after the Milan gathering, Fr Hurley and
his friends pondered and prayed about how the Italian
version of cells could be adapted in an Irish context.
They decided to put the emphasis on evangelisation
and serving people they met every day, rather than
concentrating on the quality of the group meeting. In
Italy the cell groups met weekly. Father Hurley and his
group proposed fortnightly meetings, so that people
would have more time between the cell gatherings to
connect to others and serve them.

They ran an introductory course in Ballinteer. Forty-
six people came. To their surprise, more than half said
they would like to be part of a cell group. 'There and then
we had four groups,' said Fr Hurley. At the start couples
lead the groups, but as the cells grew and multiplied,
many groups were hosted by single people, or people
who were married but whose spouse was not involved.

They also tried to involve young people, and after a few years they had up to eighty sixteen to eighteen-year-olds involved in cell groups.

From Ballinteer, the cell system spread to parishes in Longford, Tipperary, Carrickfergus, Belfast, Whiteabbbey, Newtownards, Leitrim, Kilkenny and Leixlip.

When Fr Hurley left Ballinteer parish in 1996, he wondered would the cell system continue without him: 'I was looking over my shoulder, anxious to see if it would survive my going.' It did. Today the cells are still 'a vibrant part of the parish,' Jo Gleeson tells me. She is a member of one of the ten parish cells. 'The cell means everything to me in terms of the faith support that is there through thick and thin, in hard and joyful times,' she says.

Her cell group meets in her home. She sees it as a 'wonderful grace'. 'I feel our home has been blessed. All of life is brought confidentially into that room on a Wednesday night. Graces flow and we receive gratefully.'

Parish cells grow organically. Initially a small number of interested parishioners go to a *Come and See* programme hosted by practiced cell members. If they are interested, they attend a cell group in another parish. When they decide to host a cell group, one or two experienced members join them and then return to their own groups when the new group is established. Large groups divide in two, and more people are invited to join.

Thomas and Bridie Clancy, who host a cell group in Leixlip, came from traditional Catholic backgrounds and were quite involved in the parish, but they freely admit that their faith was still a private matter. When they began to host the cell gathering, this changed.

'For the first time we could talk about our faith like people from other religions do. Ours had become so private it went into oblivion,' Thomas tells me. 'Before that, faith was going to church, listening, keeping quiet and getting out as quickly as you could.'

Thomas grew up in a border county, where the Bible was seen as a Protestant book, while in Bridie's home they only took it out at Easter and Christmas. Attending the *Come and See* programme and a cell gathering in Ballinteer helped Bridie develop a personal relationship with Jesus. 'He came into my life alive, and I understood that he would love me always and was not a punishing God.'

At the point when Bridie and Thomas began their own group in 2004, their four children were grown up and ready to leave home. At a time that could have been difficult for them, a whole new freshness entered their relationship as they began to pray together and share spiritual insights. After a while one daughter remarked, 'I never thought religion could be so much fun!'

They invited friends, work colleagues and neighbours to join them. A neighbour, Ann, from Zimbabwe, tells me she has discovered 'the community [feeling] of Africa' again at the cell gathering.

The cell system of evangelisation began in Leixlip when Fr Michael Hurley was appointed parish priest. He believes they make a huge contribution to parish life. 'Something happens when people sit down together to pray. Their own prayer is awakened, and they very quickly find a way of expressing it and contributing to parish life.'

He sees the cell group gathering as the ideal training group for service in the parish, whether in ministry, like reading or distributing communion, or, in particular, in visiting people's homes. Most of all, though, the groups bridge the gap between faith and life. 'That is what evangelisation is – helping people to recognise the connection of their own life with God.'

Father Hurley has now left the parish, but the cells continue to grow. 'They have a life and momentum of their own,' says Thomas. Today there are fourteen groups in Leixlip, including one for young adults (hosted by Thomas and Bridie's daughter), two morning groups (for young mothers) and two all-male groups.

'We have to go back to basics,' says Thomas 'and become real Christians'. He and Bridie are not perplexed by the dark period the Church is living in Ireland. 'There have always been times when the Church gets into great difficulty, but they can become times of reform and change. I have hope and I invoke the Holy Spirit for the future of the Church. We do not have anything to fear,' Bridie says.

# Powerhouse of the Spirit: Charismatic Renewal

RITA STOOD AT THE KITCHEN SINK CRYING. HER husband was an alcoholic. She had six children, the youngest aged ten. She was close to despair. Then she heard a voice whispering inside, 'Go to the prayer meeting.' She went to the local Charismatic group, and almost immediately began to experience healing, even through the words of the songs. A man in the group who had suffered with alcohol addiction offered to meet her husband and pray with him. Days later, he brought him to Alcoholics Anonymous. 'He only went to one or two AA meetings and then he stopped drinking. He never drank again,' Rita tells me.

As a child, Celine was abused by a family member. She covered it up, had counselling and got on with her life. But the hurt remained. Years later, she went to a Charismatic *Life in the Spirit* seminar. 'I realised I was a child of God. That gave me a dignity that no one could take from me. It did me a huge good – more than all the counselling.'

Mary, a civil servant, was broken-hearted when her marriage ended. She had a six-year-old daughter at the time. She felt totally alone. A friend invited her to a meeting where a Charismatic Renewal priest would speak. She went. After a time she felt the 'black cloud lifting and joy being poured into my heart.' Regular prayer meetings gave her peace and joy. 'I felt the Lord was in this [the experience of the marriage breakup].

There was a bigger plan. The words from Joel 2:25 consoled me: "I will repay you for the years the locusts have eaten ..."'

Three stories, three women, one prayer group in Chapelizod, Dublin. This group has been meeting continuously since 1976. People have come and prayed, stayed or gone. Some have died but they are not forgotten.

On a breezy Wednesday night in September, I join their meeting at Mount Sackville Convent. Twelve people sit in a circle. They know each other well. There is love and acceptance. The meeting is loosely structured around praise, singing, the reading of Scripture, testimony (or a person's understanding of what they have read), a brief teaching and petitions and announcements. It lasts about two hours. During the praises, several people speak in tongues. This sounds like a harmonious babbling that combines random note and word sounds and apparently brings people into a deeper level of prayer. I'm pretty musical and I'd like to add to the harmonies, but I can't do it. It has to come from God.

Patricia is praying in tongues at our meeting. I ask her about the experience. 'Tongues is a gift of prayer that allows you to focus on the Giver of the gift rather than yourself, and opens you to God's action in your life.'

What does it feel like? 'I experience that I'm giving glory to God and a great peace comes.' Not everyone in Renewal prays in this way, she says, but most do.

Another key feature of the Renewal is Baptism in the Spirit, described as a 'religious experience which initiates a decisively new sense of the presence of and working of God in one's life', and usually involves 'one or more charismatic gifts'.[47]

---

47. Frank Sullivan, *Baptism in the Holy Spirit*, *Gregorianum* Journal, 1974.

It was probably seeing this manifestation of praying in tongues and Baptism in the Spirit that made the Catholic Church initially so nervous about the movement when it came onto the scene in the late 1960s.

Unlike other movements, Renewal does not have a founder. At different times and in disparate places, people experienced an outpouring of the Holy Spirit when they prayed in a particular way. Cardinal Leon Joseph Suenens, an early champion of Charismatic Renewal, described it as 'pentecostal grace'. Years later the preacher to the Papal household, Fr Raniero Cantalamessa OFM Cap., explained the phenomenon in terms of a direct intervention by the Trinity: 'It seemed to me that I could perceive what new thing the Lord was doing in the Church through the Renewal,' he said. 'I wrote "The Father wants to glorify His Son Jesus Christ on earth in a new way, with a new invention. The Holy Spirit has been charged with this glorification. A Christian life totally consecrated to God, without a founder, nor rules, nor new congregations. Founder: Jesus Christ; Rule: the Gospel interpreted by the Holy Spirit; Congregation: the Church."'[48]

The earliest accounts of this outpouring of the Holy Spirit date back to the turn of the twentieth century. On 1 January 1901, Agnes Ozman suggested to her Methodist minister that he and a group of people at a Bible school in Topeka, Kansas, should lay hands on her as described in the Acts of the Apostles. Immediately she began to speak in tongues and experienced what came to be known as Baptism in the Spirit. Her Minister, Charles Parham, a Methodist, realised they had found something valuable, and preached about it. From this the

---

48. *Good News* magazine, May/June 2008.

Pentecostal Church was born. It soon became the fastest growing denomination but was sharply divided from other churches.

By the 1960s, the mainline Protestant Churches began to have members with 'Pentecostal'-style gifts, who this time remained within their denominations.

In 1967 a group of faculty and students from the Catholic Duquesne University, Pittsburgh, gathered for a weekend retreat centred on the first four chapters of the Acts of the Apostles. All present experienced God working deeply within their spirits and charismatic gifts were manifested in the group. They talked of a 'baptism in the Holy Spirit' but did not consider this as a replacement of the sacraments of baptism and confirmation. One of them wrote: 'It seemed rather a kind of adult re-affirmation and renewal of these sacramental graces.'[49]

Cardinal Suenens, one of the four moderators of the Second Vatican Council, describes how the whole experience at Duquesne University spontaneously spread to other universities. 'A remarkable thing has happened; without any mutual contact, it seems that the Spirit has initiated, in various parts of the world, experiences which, if not identical, are at least comparable.'[50]

The cardinal informed the then pope, Paul VI, of the current that was 'spreading with prodigious speed' in the five continents, and shortly after was given special pastoral responsibility for the Renewal. Although the Catholic Church only approved the statutes of the central structure of International Catholic Charismatic Renewal Services (ICCRS), in 1993, different popes have

---

49. K. and D. Ranaghan, *Catholic Pentecostals* (New Jersey: Paulist Press, 1969), p. 7.

50. Ibid., p. 76.

long recognised its spiritual force as a gift for the whole Church, beginning with Pope Paul VI.

In 1975 he addressed a large group of Catholic Charismatic leaders at St Peter's Square. The Pope spoke of three points of discernment that should be used with regard to the Movements. The first of these guidelines was fidelity of the authentic doctrine of the faith;[51] the second was that all spiritual gifts were to be received with gratitude for the common good, that is to build up the whole Church and society; and the third and most important of all was that it was only the love of charity, *agape*, that made Christians perfect.

Charismatic Renewal, which he described as a 'chance for the Church and the world', ought to 'rejuvenate the world, give it back a spirituality, a soul, a religious thought. It ought to reopen its closed lips to prayer and open its mouth to song, to joy, to hymns and to witnessing.'[52]

In Ireland, Charismatic Renewal broke onto the scene over forty years ago, in January 1971. Since then it has transformed the lives of thousands of people, helping them experience the power of prayer and the gifts of the Holy Spirit, going from, as Mary told me, 'a ritualistic faith to an expectant faith'.

'Renewal is not a movement', says Patricia, who helps run *Life in the Spirit* seminars. 'It is the grace of the Holy Spirit that perpetuates Baptism and Confirmation and brings you fully into the life of the Church'.

In its exciting early days, every Friday night in Eustace Street in Dublin, six hundred people attended their prayer meeting. Over twenty-five thousand people attended the International Conference in 1978 in the RDS. As time

---

51. Cf. 1 Cor 1–3.

52. Pope Paul VI to Conference on the Catholic Charismatic Renewal, 19 May 1975.

passed, the character of Charismatic Renewal changed. Streams of spirituality influenced by, for example, Medjugorje or Divine Mercy, entered the prayer groups, which became more Catholic (although members of other denominations or of none are welcome).

Paul VI's appeal to 'go back to the heart of the Church' was taken by many as a call to immerse themselves in their local parish communities. Many explored other forms of prayer like Eucharistic Adoration. Others formed their own communities and schools of evangelisation – a multiplicity of fruits all flowing from an experience of the Spirit.

Today there are three hundred prayer groups in the country, eighty in the Dublin archdiocese alone. Every June its annual conference attracts 1,600 people. The age profile is generally older now, but young people come too. Ashley, aged twenty-five, was at our meeting in Chapelizod. A student of International Business, he made contact with the group leader, Bernie, through her brother, a priest in Zimbabwe. 'Initially I asked myself: "What am I doing here?"' he told me. 'Then I realised it was not about age, but what I was getting from it.' Recently he's faced visa problems and unemployment. The prayer group prays with him, and supports him emotionally to accept whatever happens. 'I receive a lot and I leave refreshed. It lifts me up,' he tells me.

Kathy agrees. For years she has been supported through difficult trials at her prayer meeting. Abandoned by an alcoholic mother as a baby, Kathy grew up in an orphanage run by some loving nuns, the Daughters of the Heart of Mary. At sixteen she left, and began her own life. After marrying and having children, at age thirty-two, out of the blue, she began to experience dreadful panic attacks. A psychiatrist prescribed medication. 'I felt trapped,' she told me, thinking she would be sedated for the rest of her life. A few years later, a friend invited her to Medjugorje, where she experienced great healing. She realised that her panic attacks stemmed from her experience of abandonment as a child, and that she needed to forgive her mother. On her return to Ireland, she visited her GP and asked him to wean her off the pills. She felt she was cured. She was.

Kathy began to go to a weekly prayer meeting. Through the Renewal, she was guided to 'pray through her family tree' to find the peace and acceptance she needed so much.

Ten years ago her husband developed a brain tumour. Another painful experience began, with treatments, his loss of mobility and a paralysing uncertainty about the future. But Kathy is not for crumbling. Her faith in prayer and the support of her Charismatic Renewal friends make her strong. 'I don't know what I would do without the fellowship. It carries you through when you can't pray yourself. You know others are praying for you and that keeps you going.'

# =8=

# Witnessing Christian Marriage: Teams of Our Lady

WHEN FOUR RECENTLY MARRIED COUPLES APPROACHED a priest in Paris in 1939, asking him to help them live their newfound love in the light of faith, his reply was, 'Let us journey together'. This was the start of the Equipes Notre-Dame, or Teams of Our Lady, which has now spread to seventy-five countries, involving over 120,000 people and bringing out the powerful vocation of Christian marriage.

On a cold winter's night I went to visit the Team in West Dublin. It had been a hard day. I'd spent seven hours in casualty waiting with a sick relative, while ambulances delivered crash victims, a raffish drunk lectured us on the economy and the walking wounded patiently marked time in the waiting room.

Now it was evening and I was at the door of Mary and Hugo Gallagher's house in Leixlip. I was frazzled and late! Mary warmly welcomed me into a cosy sitting room where four couples and a priest were saying a few prayers around a candle. They greeted me, and we settled down to pray. Immediately I felt enveloped by the peace. Father John O'Keefe, a Jesuit priest, led the prayer and spoke about appreciating the treasure of faith in each person, including those of non-Christian faith. In moments of silence, you could hear the ticking clock in the hall and the hissing of the gas fire. After the silence, each person prayed a petition.

Then we adjourned to the dining room to eat and quell our rumbling tummies. Each couple had brought their own meal, which made it very easy for everyone. Our hosts supplied a meal for Fr John, but in other groups, the priest brings along his own tea – each group suits itself.

As we ate, each person in turn shared what they had lived in the previous month – their experiences of meeting God. They pooled stories of bereavement, business problems, emigration, illnesses, exam pressures financial worries and family joys.

This year Joe and Áine are leading the Leixlip group. (Leadership rotates, as does the location for their monthly meeting.) 'We help one another. There's a friendship, but also a code of confidentiality. People are free to say anything and be sure it won't go outside the room,' Áine tells me.

Tonight a new couple is sitting in (like me) to get a feel for the movement and find out if it is for them. Father John, who works as a chaplain in St Vincent's Hospital, shares too, and it is a strong moment of dialogue showing the beauty of both vocations – marriage and the celibate life.

He moved to Dublin in 2005 and joined this team. 'It is a faith support for me,' he tells me between courses, 'I receive much more than I give.'

The Equipes Notre-Dame was started by Fr Henri Caffarel in Paris in 1939, just before Europe was engulfed by the Second World War. Years earlier, in 1923, aged twenty, the young Henri had a strong experience of the personal love of God for him. 'Jesus Christ, in a flash became Somebody for me. Oh! It was nothing spectacular. On that day in March, now far distant, I knew that I was loved and that I loved, and that henceforth between him and me it would be for life. The die was cast,' he wrote, describing the event that was to change his life.[53]

In 1930 he was ordained a priest, and began to dedicate his time to the spiritual formation of lay Christians, especially young people. In time these young people married and came to him for advice on their marital life. In 1939 he gathered together a number of couples and invited them to seek, together with him, a way of sanctity for couples. Little by little he developed a spirituality based on the sacrament of marriage. The groups of couples, known at the time as the Caffarel Teams, grew larger, and to spread his ideas more widely, Fr Caffarel founded a journal called the *Golden Ring*.

He saw the sacrament of marriage as a way to holiness. 'A true Christian home is a work of God, the brilliance of the sacrament of marriage is the reflection of the immense tenderness uniting Christ to the Church.'[54]

His spirituality of marriage was not built on a monastic style of life, but rather on the state of life of marriage, with all its needs, difficulties and grace. He invited couples to live as one single love – their conjugal love and their love of Christ.

The whole of family life had to be Christian, he said. 'Ask yourself: deep down, what does God think of love, of fatherhood and motherhood, sexuality, education, what does he think about all the important realities of the home?'[55] He called for a 'Christian style' of relationships between family members, a Christian framework for the home affecting practical things like meals or how people spent money and a Christian style of daily activities.

53. Cited in *Père Henri Caffarel, apôtre de la spiritualité conjugale*, Eric Madre at www.mavocation.org.

54. Ibid.

55. *Golden Ring* magazine, Issue 84.

'How can you act so that all of this is Christian, appears as Christian, that it shines with Christ's grace?' he asked.[56]

The Caffarel teams multiplied after the war, nationally and internationally. This led to the drawing up of a charter in 1947 which presented its essential objectives as a worldwide Christian movement for married couples, seeking to develop their relationship with God personally and as a couple.

Based on this charter, the movement crossed many country and language boundaries and became known by a new name: Equipes Notre-Dame, a name which was then translated into different languages as the movement spread. The Teams of Our Lady grew rapidly in France, Belgium and Switzerland. In the 1950s the movement crossed the world to North and South America and Africa, while extending in mainland Europe as far as Italy and the UK. By the 1960s, it had reached Australia, Japan, India, Vietnam and the Middle East. Today there are teams in over seventy countries.

Father Caffarel remained closely bound to the teams of Our Lady until he was seventy years of age, when he retired from active service in the organisation, but he continued to introduce Christians to prayer at his prayer school in Troussures. He died in 1996 in Troussures, where he is buried. At his funeral Mass, Cardinal Jean-Marie Lustiger described him as a prophet of the twentieth century. The process of his beatification is going ahead.

The Equipes Notre-Dame reached Ireland in 1964. An Irish couple met a French Jesuit who introduced them to an Irish priest who had met the teams in France. A year after their meeting the first team meeting took place

---

56. Ibid.

in Ireland, helped by a more experienced couple from the UK. The Irish teams were part of the Teams in Great Britain until 1974, when it became a separate region.

Today there are thirty-two teams, each involving four to six couples, spread across the country in Galway, Mullingar, Limerick, Belfast, Sligo, Meath and Dublin. Worldwide it is a single international movement with 122,000 members, all striving to be renewed in their marriages and to help each other. Teams are grouped into sectors, regions and super regions.

The life of a Team of Our Lady is based around the original Charter written by Henri Caffarel in 1947. It proposed six 'endeavours' to help them grow in their love for God, individually and as couples: personal prayer, conjugal and family prayer; regular dialogue in the sight of God as a couple (the Sit Down); daily Scripture reading; a personal rule of life; and an annual spiritual retreat.

At every gathering, the team considers one of these 'endeavours' in more depth.

The evening I spent with the Leixlip group, they focused on the Sit Down. This is a period of time that each couple sets aside, where in the presence of God they try to look at their lives together.

Joe, originally from Manchester, talked about how the Sit Down taught him to 'shut up and listen!' Everyone laughed. Áine, his wife of thirty-seven years, nodded, adding, 'It is very valuable. It is different to other times we're together.'

Tony, who works in tourism, described the process. 'A couple sit down and are quiet. If a thing is on your mind, you discuss it frankly and openly. There's a great sense of peace. It is like you've had a meeting with God.'

His wife Breda, a nurse, said it reminded her of confession. 'You get a feeling of relief and inner peace.'

Some couples find the Sit Down more difficult than others, but at this meeting, they all agreed it was a precious moment.

During the final part of the meeting the team discussed the chapter of a spiritual book they are studying in between meetings – *The Naked Now* by Richard Rohr. There is no attempt to reach consensus or a conclusion, merely to exchange understandings. At the end, they stood to recite the Magnificat – a worthy end to the evening.

While for years the growth of the movement was slow, in the last few years it has experienced new life with the birth of five new teams. Up to this time the movement spread mostly through personal contact, but in more recent years they have begun to advertise at pre-marriage courses and parish retreats, and through this, young couples, thirsty for a spirituality in their marriages, have entered the movement.

The couples in the Leixlip team came to the movement through the invitation of a friend. Breda, for example, was nursing with Mary. 'I thought it was a lovely way to meet people,' says Breda, but her husband Tony found it harder at the start. 'I was reticent about sharing. It took time to build up trust.'

The couples, all of whom have large extended families, said the movement brings them closer to God and each other. 'You realise the Holy Spirit is so present in your life,' says Breda. For Tony it has brought a new love of Scripture. 'I was always a devout Catholic, but I didn't have a strong understanding of Scriptures. I feel I've gained great riches from reading Scripture and a closeness to God.'

Moments of profound unity with each other stand out as the gems in their marriage. One weekend the couple were at Old Trafford for a Manchester United match. Afterwards, back at the hotel, they had a Sit Down session. 'I couldn't describe it. The sense of peace,' Tony says, adding with a laugh, 'Of course we won, though I don't think that had much to do with it!'

The Teams of Our Lady also has a Rule of Life. This can be a task, a chore or a prayer that a member will undertake to do for a whole year.

When the children leave home and couples are left alone, it can be a challenging time. Some even admit to a sense of panic. 'What will we talk about?' But the team's spirituality makes this a time of great enrichment.

'We pray together as a couple. We study Scripture together, we go through the team's Rule of Life, together and separately. It has brought us many steps down the road and we've grown spiritually,' says Joe.

The prayer and friendship among the couples is a bedrock support to each one, especially in times of trial. 'When we're all together, there is not one issue or worry affecting families that is not covered, and yet we are still praising God. You are a team. It is a family,' says Mary.

# =9=
# Covenant People:
# The Community of Nazareth

IN THE 1970S, IN DUBLIN, A SMALL GROUP OF Charismatic Renewal couples cast about for a group that would also involve their children. They had tried prayer groups and movements for married couples, but they wanted something more.

Éanna and Pat Johnson heard of a community in New Jersey and decided, together with their four teenage children, to pay them a visit. They were impressed by what they saw.

The community, the People of Hope, was a covenant community – a religious group whose members bound themselves to one another and to the group by a solemn agreement or covenant.

'It was an opportunity to personally experience the lived reality of this concept of charismatic covenant community,' says Éanna. 'The response of each and every member of the family was very positive, so I began to think that maybe this was indeed the way the Lord was calling us.'

They came back with a new vision.

In 1984, it seemed the time was right for a similar type of community in Ireland. At a retreat in Ballyvaloo in Wexford, nine married couples, three young single people and a priest decided they would come together to form a lay 'covenant community' – one of the first such in Ireland – which in time was named the Community of Nazareth.

On a mild day in Dún Laoghaire, I meet two members of Dublin's community, Brendan Lynch (who, with his wife, Caitriona, was one of the earliest members of the Community of Nazareth), and Adrian Buckley (who came to it later). Brendan is currently the senior coordinator of the group. He works as an actuary and we sit in his office.

The Community of Nazareth has four main aspects: life with God, with one another, witness and service in society.

When it started there were around twenty adults and twenty-five children. Practically, they agreed to meet regularly enough so that they could live out the solemn covenant which each member had declared, taking 'responsibility for the brothers and sisters whom the Lord has given us in our new family and to work together in Christian fellowship for the fulfilment of the mission he has entrusted to us.'

At the beginning, three of the families were neighbours, living in an estate in Ballybrack, so the area became the natural hub of the community. As it grew, others moved to the estate or close by.

Today, the community numbers two hundred, half being made up of children.

Adrian Buckley, sitting beside me in Brendan's office, came from a family that was involved in Marriage Encounter. Studying architecture in UCD, he went to a charismatic *Life in the Spirit* seminar and for the first time discovered his own personal relationship with Jesus, and decided to live in a new way.

Restructuring his life took time. 'I started to read the Bible and understood the Holy Spirit was present there. You didn't have to live your life on your own,' he tells me.

After six months, Adrian asked to become an 'underway' member of the community. Sometime later he met Aisling, who was linked to another covenant community in Brussels. A year later they married.

According to Adrian, community life is very supportive of family life. 'It is a tremendous blessing for our family. For the children, for example, it is a great opportunity to have the possibility of being in a daily relationship with other young people who have a similar sense of faith and are a positive peer group,' he says.

He believes that the special gift of the Community of Nazareth is as a place where families can share and live together, although the community also has lots of single people who try to live a more committed life in God's service, guided by the Holy Spirit.

The Community of Nazareth is a Catholic community which is open to all and with a heart for ecumenism and for Christian unity. In any community there is always a danger that it can become turned in on itself. Not so with Nazareth, which acquires a broad breadth of vision and life through its link to Sword of the Spirit – a grouping of seventy-plus full-member covenant communities and up to one hundred other related communities.

Scattered across Europe, Asia and America, each of these member communities is self-governing, but they all share a common vision and mission. Young people from close-by communities (like Brussels, Glasgow and London) get together each year for friendship and support. In Ireland there are two communities, the Community of Nazareth, and in Belfast the Charis Community. In all, about 10,000 people are involved in these covenant communities worldwide.

The link between the communities is very strong, says Caitriona Lynch. 'We see ourselves as brother and sister communities around the world.'

Community members live normal lives centred around family, work and study. What is different, Brendan explains to me, is the 'pattern of life' central to their commitment to the Lord. These are special moments when they put time aside to meet. For example, the whole community meets twice a month on a Sunday afternoon in a parish hall. At the two-hour gathering there is prayer and praise, teaching on Scripture, testimony and celebration of special days in community members' lives, like birthdays and anniversaries.

I popped along to one of these gatherings to get to know the wider group. On a warm Sunday in May, I joined about 150 people of all ages who thronged the parish hall in Johnstown. A band featuring a guitarist, keyboard player, drummer, violinist and a singer lead the music which had everyone standing and singing for the first part of the afternoon. Then young children went to their own programmes. Brendan Lynch gave a teaching on the day's Scripture, and after a time the young people returned. They had been studying some stories from the Old Testament – the story of Creation, Adam and Eve, Noah's Ark, the Tower of Babel and the story of Joseph. Two young people, Scott and Eoin, turned the stories into funny sketches in rhyme, which about twenty of the children acted out in sequence using a wide side-window ledge as a platform. We all turned our chairs to the left to face the windows and makeshift stage. It was great fun and yet the message of each story was coming through and the children would clearly remember them.

Before we left there was a sharing of local news – a remembering of friends who were sick or in hospital, anniversaries and birthdays. Naomi, an eighteen year old about to sit her Leaving Cert, shared her excitement over organising a three-month trip to Germany to work with a Christian group combating human trafficking. After a final song the meeting broke up. People chatted in small groups, and those with particular concerns went for 'healing prayer' to a smaller room where they prayed together with others.

The young people would meet again on Friday night at the NYPD – Nazareth Youth Programme Dublin – for their own programmes. The NYPD caters for four age groups: Juniors (second to fourth class – aged seven to nine years), Middle (fifth and sixth class – aged ten to eleven years), Senior (first to third year – twelve to fourteen years) and Young Adult (fourth to sixth year – sixteen to eighteen years).

My informant on the NYPD is Aoife, Adrian's eldest daughter, who describes the Friday night youth club as 'chill time to be with everyone and to share our difficulties'.

She is with the young adult group, and there are fifteen of them. Sometimes they have a guest speaker. 'It is a great support for me because I have a lot of friends my age in the Community of Nazareth and they have the same beliefs as me. We chat away and sometimes the smallest things can uplift you.'

While the Buckley family has been part of the Community of Nazareth since Aoife was four, she admits that it's only recently that she's been a real believer. 'I've only had a real relationship with God over the last few years.' She expresses that faith with a time of personal prayer in the morning and by treating each person she meets 'the same'.

A simple but special family time is at 7 a.m. over breakfast each morning, when Adrian, her father, reads the Gospel of the day from an app on his phone. 'I don't know anyone else who does it, but it's always been there and it's a nice family time for about five minutes in the morning, in all the chaos of "pass me the milk" and "where's my homework?"' says Aoife.

She is studying for her Leaving in a Gaelscoil in Stillorgan. She's not embarrassed to be part of a Christian community, and is ready to tell her school friends about her faith if she's asked. 'I tell them it's living a better life trying to follow God's word,' she says.

When young people turn eighteen they have the opportunity to choose to become 'underway members' in their own right. The 'underway period' is a period of discipleship that lasts a few years. During that time, the underway member is involved in a small sharing group and receives a series of teachings and one-on-one support from a member. Usually as the time progresses it becomes clear to the person if they are called to be a full member (which involves, for example, some level of service to the community, and sharing a proportion of their income) or if they prefer to try something different.

About 40 per cent choose to stay in the community, continuing to share in each other's lives as a group of single people, and meeting regularly in small, single-sex sharing groups.

According to Ann Byrne, one of the original members of Nazareth, the charism of the community is family. 'A lot of us were connected with Teams of Our Lady and were involved in some marriage counselling, and when we started the community we thought its gift would be to support marriage, but really the gift is for family life.' The community actually manages to hold onto young people. Many of the children have become part of the community, and now a second generation (the grandchildren of the founders of Nazareth) are also involved.

But it would be wrong to think that belonging to the Community of Nazareth just involves attending a series of gatherings. They do meet regularly, and some live close to each other, but the community aims to be a real sharing of life and they try to support each other practically.

'If someone had a baby, we'd cook a dinner one night and another person would do it another night,' Aoife cites as an example. Of course they experience the same pains and problems as everyone else, but go beyond them through faith and through mutual support.

Adrian's family has been hit hard by the economic downturn. Three years ago his biggest client went into receivership, owing a lot of money. 'The weight we've had to work through has been managing financially and steering the business through that turbulent time,' he tells me, 'but my commitment to the Lord, my sense of blessing from the Lord and his provision for me has carried us through.'

The members of Nazareth try to help each other financially too if the need arises. The need is shared in a confidential manner, and in the same 'confidential manner' others try to help.

In Adrian's house, where the whole family is part of the community, peace reigns.

'Really?' I ask Aoife. 'No rows? No slamming doors?'

'We don't really have family rows,' she tells me sincerely. 'Sometimes I get annoyed at my sister for staying too long in the bathroom, but that's about it.'

And while she has experienced moments of rebellion, she has also realised that without friends and support, 'life is hard'. Better still, she has understood through her family, and through being part of a vibrant Christian community, that following the plan that God has for her is a 'journey of discovery – trying to discover where you're meant to be in order to live to your full potential'.

# ≡10≡
## Youth 2000

'YOU'LL RECOGNISE ME BY MY RED HAIR,' I TOLD HER when I set up the interview. 'Oh, I have red hair too,' she replied, 'in the front.' I was puzzled. When I met her I knew exactly what she meant. Maura Garrihy was not joking. A streak of luminous scarlet hair slashed across her forehead.

For the next hour we chatted in a café in Maynooth and she told me about Youth 2000, the movement that has completely changed her life.

In her own words, she came from a family with 'hardcore' Catholic values, but although she was always interested in faith, she did not have a relationship with God. Her Junior Cert year at school was a raw one. Her beloved grandmother died, and shortly afterwards an uncle. She was close to both, especially her granny, but as she was sitting the Junior Cert at the time, there was no time to grieve. On the outside everything was fine, but inside there was a big wound.

In Transition Year the school chaplain at her school in Ennistymon invited her to a Youth 2000 weekend retreat in Ennis. Her first experience on the Friday evening was a 'happy clappy' Mass. 'What have I got myself into?' she asked herself. Straight after the Mass she rang her dad and asked him to come and collect her. He told her to give it a chance, so she stayed. She began to notice the joy of the people around her. 'It didn't fit in with my idea of the Church and God.' She wanted the same thing. 'For the first time I opened up.' It was a deeply emotional experience. She cried a lot that weekend, but it was a turning point. She realised she had a decision to make – she could keep on living a life of pretence, or she could accept that God loved her and surrender to that relationship. She chose God. 'I went back home and people were asking me, "What is wrong. You're awfully happy!"' When she returned to school, she told her friends about the retreat and so began her new life. Over the following year, a lot of inner turmoil was resolved – including the deep-seated loss of a twin brother who had died at birth. 'I opened my mind and heart to God and gave him 100 per cent. I processed all these issues through the retreats, the prayer meetings and faith friends.'

The experience of meeting God in such a profound way planted a deep thirst for knowledge of religion in Maura, and when she left school, she decided to study theology (and business) at Maynooth. Arriving to study, she was immediately part of the Youth 2000 family there who looked out for her.

Maura's experience demonstrates how Youth 2000 works. First of all, it is young people who evangelise young people. In fact, it was the words of Pope John Paul II that inspired Englishman Ernest Williams to start the movement. 'It is to you young people that the task first falls of bearing witness to the faith and of bringing into the third millennium the Gospel of Christ, who is the Way, the Truth and the Life,' Pope John Paul II had told the young people at the World Youth meeting in Santiago de Compostela in Spain in 1989. In response, Ernest, a twenty-six-year-old IT specialist, began to gather young people together in prayer, and soon the initiative, known as Youth 2000, spread to more than twenty-five countries all over the world. It reached Ireland in 1993.

Typically a young person will be invited to a retreat, often by a friend. 'It is just mad. Where else can you have something in common between someone in Transition Year and someone who has been working for ten years?' asks Maura. Youth 2000 holds sixteen to eighteen retreats a year all over the country. Afterwards, young people can go to a local prayer meeting if they wish (forty weekly venues in Ireland). Currently there are thousands of young people involved and, according to Maura, the movement is going from strength to strength.

I went to one of their prayer meetings – in the heart of Dublin at the Blessed Sacrament Chapel, Bachelor's Walk. It was coming up to the summer holidays, so a smaller group gathered to pray. But still, on a sunny evening in Dublin when most young people in their twenties were in the pub or basking in some rare sunshine on the Liffey boardwalk outside, about thirty young people gathered to pray. Most were students, many from the nearby Trinity College Dublin.

The meeting began when one of the Blessed Sacrament Fathers, Fr Raphael, processed in carrying the Blessed Sacrament in a monstrance while those present sang the theme song from the Eucharistic Congress, 'Though We are Many'. For a few minutes everyone sat or knelt in silence before the Eucharist, and then the Rosary began. This was recited slowly and reverently. Between each decade, we sang a verse from a traditional song, like an Ave, and then someone read a passage from the Gospel relating to the next mystery. It was Tuesday night, so we were meditating on the sorrowful mysteries. At the end of the Rosary a period of silent Eucharistic Adoration began.

Although we were in the heart of Dublin city, there was a dense silence. The only sound was the quiet hum of the air conditioning. Many of the young people were kneeling, some on their hunkers. It was profoundly moving to see their devoutness.

Before Fr Raphael gave a talk, they sang a beautiful song with many harmonies, 'Lord, You have My Heart', accompanied by keyboard and guitar. The Eucharistic Congress had just finished, so Fr Raphael shared his own impressions of the week, in particular the strong 'sense of community' that was evident between everyone, whether cardinal, bishop or child.

At the end of Fr Raphael's talk, there was more song, announcements and a welcome cup of tea and a biscuit.

Katie Lally from Swords, one of the singers, told me she had been coming to the prayer group since September. 'It makes Jesus more present in my life. It opens you up to him,' she told me. Katie's interest in faith grew through music in the parish, where she was involved in various choirs. Now she's studying in Mater Dei to be a religious education teacher.

Timothé from France was in Ireland for the summer. He had heard about Youth 2000 in Paris. 'I had heard of all the problems in the Irish Church. I was surprised to find such an alive group. The love and joy changed me. I feel an incredible peace.' Timothé grew up in a strong Catholic family but over time his older brothers and sisters fell away from practising their faith. He was inclined to follow them. 'They were all saying "No!" Then I looked back [at my life] and said "What am I doing?" I realised the importance of my faith.'

According to Ryan Connolly, twenty-one, the people who come to their prayer meeting are mostly already interested in faith. He is studying English literature in TCD. 'For people moving to Dublin from other parts of the country or from abroad, they find great support here.' Was it a challenge to live his faith at college, I asked him. 'As long as I have support, I don't find it a struggle. It is difficult on your own, like when I was at school.'

Ryan initially made contact with Youth 2000 when a friend invited him to a social in a pub. Then he was invited to a prayer group. He was just about to start at Trinity. 'I hadn't realised there was a faith community like this in Ireland.' Before he went to college, he attended the group's summer festival in Clonmacnoise, a gathering of around 1,000 young people. 'It was an experience to see so many young people into faith.'

I left the prayer meeting full of hope and joy. As I walked along the Liffey boardwalk a short distance away, I ran into a bunch of young people the same age as those I'd just left in the room beside the Blessed Sacrament Chapel. A lad with his head in his hands sat on a bench, surrounded by crushed empty cider cans. Others wandered around looking dazed, their eyes glazed over. It was a striking contrast.

In Youth 2000, the X Factor generation rediscover the jewels of their Catholic faith – the Eucharist and adoration, prayer and the Rosary, Scripture and the tradition of the Church.

Adoration has a profound effect on them. 'Jesus enters the room and sits among us since he is truly present in the Blessed Sacrament,' says Emma Sisk from Michelstown, studying arts in Limerick.

'I sometimes feel his love powerfully in the presence of the Blessed Sacrament, overcoming my resentment and lack of love and softening my heart again,' says Diarmuid Clifford from Galway. On the Youth 2000 website, Diarmuid tells of how he put himself under huge pressure to achieve, feeling that this was the only measure of his worth. His world came crashing down when he developed a bad stammer. 'For a while it seemed like a disaster, but eventually it forced me to re-evaluate the whole way I was living my life,' he writes. Gradually he learnt to let go and to pray, and felt raised up from the 'darkness of despair'. 'He [Jesus] has taught me to surrender, to be humble enough to accept that his plans, and not mine, bring about happiness.'

Our Lady of Guadalupe is a patron saint of Youth 2000 and the Rosary is one of their particular devotions. Usually a priest is present at their prayer meetings for spiritual direction, and he will often give spiritual input. The young people are encouraged to study the tradition of the Church – key papal encyclicals and the Catechism.

It could all sound very passé – almost like a throwback to the 1950s – if it were not for one vital component: here we are talking about modern young people who are not blindly adhering to a message because they are expected to by the Church or society, but who are making the choice for themselves, experiencing the joy of the love of God, and then witnessing it to their friends.

'We are totally living it out each day, and testifying to the love of God,' Maura tells me with passion.

Through the organisation, the young people form strong friendships with each other (which has resulted in a number of marriages), socialise through things like hill walking, the Valentine Ball, or the huge four-day summer festival at Clonmacnoise, and often individually get involved in social actions.

'Faith should not be confined to prayer. You're more of a witness if you're balanced,' says Maura, who works part-time for a surf school in Lahinch.

At a time when the Catholic Church is being buffeted by scandal after scandal, Youth 2000 grows among the people one might expect to be furthest from its message – the young. Maura says it's a 'time of purification'. 'The Church is about more than those few priests who abused. I've met the most beautiful priests. It saddens me to think they're getting the backlash. I've experienced the Church's vitality and love. The Church loves you. I couldn't be more determined to show and share this with others.'

Matthew Berkeley, a fourth-year astrophysics student in TCD agrees. 'The scandals are a scar on the face of Christ. Our job is to bring the Church back to a place that radiates the joy of Christ again.'

# ⇒ Conclusion ⇐

AS CHRISTIANS LOOKING AT TODAY'S WORLD,
sometimes we can be hit by two feelings. One is nostalgia
for the past. Looking back, it seems everything was so
simple. Everyone believed in God, people had less but
seemed happier, and faith played a big part in their
day-to-day lives. It is probably a simplistic analysis –
but we ask ourselves, 'Wasn't there more faith then and
weren't people a lot happier? Why can't we return to
the past?'

Another feeling is wanting to give up. Information
is so widespread, all-pervasive and all-consuming, that
we are barraged with bad news on a minute-by-minute
basis. Terrible deeds and ways of behaving are subjected
to minute scrutiny, and in the media feeding frenzy we
hear every last detail of a mass killer's life, of the abuse of
a child, of tumbling levels of faith and religious practice,
and feel ourselves drowning in the mire.

But the Holy Spirit is definitely at work in his Church
and in the world. And if I have learnt anything from my
foray into these ten movements, it is that he is incredibly
generous with his gifts.

God is at work as never before, and as St Paul says,
everything works for good for those who love God.[57] To
believe that the Catholic Church is in a worse state now
than it was a hundred years ago is to do a profound act of
injustice to the Holy Spirit. But we risk missing out on an
appointment with history if we ignore the gifts scattered
so generously by God throughout the world and in our
own country. He is at work in the movements, in the
new communities and in all the great people working in

---

57. Romans 8:28

parishes and in initiatives that are quietly renewing the Church.

The challenge for us Christians is to act as the people I interviewed have: listen to the voice of God, develop a one-on-one relationship with him through prayer, see where he is leading us and let him continue his transformation of the world through us. As individuals it is hard to resist the strong pull of a world where God seems airbrushed out, but when we gather together with Jesus in our midst and around the Eucharist, we can experience the strength coming from unity.

The International Eucharistic Congress in Dublin in 2012 was a wonderful opportunity to reveal to the people of the Church the extraordinary jewels it holds in its treasure chest which belong to us all. Perhaps events like this, even on a smaller scale, should be taken on in the future so we can see God's plan of love at work and rejoice in how, beyond appearances, his kingdom is advancing and in our turn have the hope and courage to 'put out into the deep.'[58]

In his encyclical letter *Novo Millennio Ineunte* – At the Dawn of the Twenty-First Century – Pope John Paul II called for a 'spirituality of communion'. And this perhaps is what is most needed today to awaken a spiritually sleepwalking world to the reality and joy of a lived Christianity. He wrote:

A spirituality of communion indicates above all the heart's contemplation of the mystery of the Trinity dwelling in us, and whose light we must also be able to see shining on the face of the brothers and sisters around us.

---

58. Luke 5:4.

> A spirituality of communion also means an ability to think of our brothers and sisters in faith within the profound unity of the Mystical Body, and therefore as 'those who are a part of me' ...
>
> A spirituality of communion implies also the ability to see what is positive in others, to welcome it and prize it as a gift from God: not only as a gift for the brother or sister who has received it directly, but also as a 'gift for me' ...

The Pope warned that external structures of communion served little purpose without this spiritual foundation. 'They would become mechanisms without a soul, "masks" of communion rather than its means of expression and growth.'[59]

In essence, a 'spirituality of communion' means all of us, as individuals and as groups, sharing out our gifts in communion with each other: the prophetic gifts of the movements in communion with the teaching gifts of the institutional Church. But this does not mean that we become the same.

As Pope John Paul II wrote in the same letter:

> The unity of the Church is not uniformity, but an organic blending of legitimate diversities. It is the reality of many members joined in a single body, the one Body of Christ (cf. 1 Cor 12:12).[60]

This was the beauty of my journey among the movements. I experienced their diversity and yet their

---

59. John Paul II, *Novo Millennio Ineunte*, 43.
60. Ibid., 46.

complementarity: each a tile in the great mosaic of the Church, each playing an indispensable role. My wish is that many people will become part of this 'springtime in the Church', wherever God calls them, so that each movement, each group, including those to come, can achieve its complete fulfilment in God's plan, bringing many people to new life and joy in him and transforming the world.

# ⇒ Contact Details ⇐

⇒ **The Legion of Mary**
De Montfort House
Morning Star Avenue
Brunswick Street
Dublin 7
Ireland
T. +353 (0) 1 872 3153
E. concilium@legion-of-mary.ie
W. www.legionofmary.ie

⇒ **Cursillo**
Termonabacca Carmelite Retreat Centre
Foyle Hill
Creegan
Derry
Coordinator: George Fitzpatrick
T. +44 (0) 28 7126 5537
Coordinator: Noel Ramsey
T. +44 (0) 28 7126 5509
E. conzo.martin@hotmail.com
W. www.cursillowalktoknock.com

⇒ **Communion and Liberation**
P.O. Box 7060
Dublin 6
Ireland
T. +353 (0) 86 8112047
E. info@clireland.com
W. www.clonline.org/ie

≡ **Focolare**
Focolare Centre
Curryhills House
Prosperous
Co. Kildare
Ireland
T. +353 (0) 45 840410 / 840420
E. info@focolare.ie
W. www.focolare.ie

≡ **L'Arche Ireland**
L'Arche Secretariat
Cluain Aoibhinn
Fairgreen Lane
Callan
Co. Kilkenny
Ireland
T. +353 (0) 56 772 5283
E. admin@larche.ie
W. www.larche.ie

≡ **Cells System of Evangelisation**
The Parish Office
St John the Evangelist Church
Ballinteer Avenue
Dublin 16
T. +353 (0) 86 3807917
E. leixlipparishcells@gmail.com
W. www.parishcellsireland.net

≡ **Catholic Charismatic Renewal**
National Service Committee (NSC)
Emmanuel
3 Pembroke Park
Ballsbridge
Dublin 4
T. +353 (0) 1 667 0570
E. nsc@iol.ie
W. www.charismaticrenewal.ie

≡ **Teams of Our Lady**
3 Elm Grove
Blackrock
Co. Dublin
T. +353 (0) 1 288 2528
E. cunneenpk@eircom.net
W. www.equipes-notre-dame.ie

≡ **The Community of Nazareth**
P.O. Box 9005
Glenageary
Co. Dublin
T. +353 (0) 86 227 2431
E.info@nazarethcommunity.org
W. www.nazarethcommunity.org

≡ **Youth 2000**
National Office
2nd Floor
Áras Treasa
Clarendon St, Dublin 2
T. +353 (0) 1 675 3690
E. dublin@youth2000.ie
W. www.youth2000.ie

# ⇒ Appendix ⇐

**DIRECTORY OF INTERNATIONAL
ASSOCIATIONS OF THE FAITHFUL**
Compiled by the Pontifical Council for the Laity

1. Adsis Communities (Adsis)
2. Amigonian Cooperators (A.Cs)
3. Apostolic Movement of Schoenstatt (Schoenstatt Movement)
4. Bread of Life Community
5. Catholic Fraternity of Charismatic Covenant Communities and Fellowships (Catholic Fraternity)
6. Catholic Integrated Community (KIG)
7. Catholic International Education Office (OIEC)
8. Chemin Neuf Community (CCN)
9. Christian Life Community (CVX)
10. Christian Life Movement (CLM)
11. Claire Amitié
12. Community of the Beatitudes
13. Comunità Domenico Tardini Association
14. Conference of International Catholic Organisations (CICO)
15. Cooperators of Opus Dei
16. Couples for Christ (CFC)
17. Emmanuel Community
18. Encounters of Married Couples (Dialogues)
19. Encounters of Youth Promotion (EYP)
20. Fondacio. Christians for the World (Fondacio)
21. Foyers de Charité
22. Fraternity of Charles de Foucauld (FCF)
23. Fraternity of Communion and Liberation (CL)

24. Fraternity of St Thomas Aquinas groups (FASTA)
25. Heart's Home
26. Heralds of the Gospel (EP)
27. Holy Family Association
28. Immaculate Heart of Mary, Mother of Mercy Association or Tuus Totus (CIM)
29. Institute for World Evangelisation (ICPE Mission)
30. Intercontinental Christian Fraternity of the Chronic Sick and Physically Disabled (FCIPMH)
31. International Alliance of Catholic Knights (IACK)
32. International Association of Caterinati
33. International Association of Charities (AIC)
34. International Association of Faith and Light
35. International Association of Missionaries of Political Charity
36. International Catholic Centre for Cooperation with UNESCO (CCIC)
37. International Catholic Centre of Geneva (ICCG)
38. International Catholic Charismatic Renewal Services (ICCRS)
39. International Catholic Child Bureau (BICE)
40. International Catholic Committee for Gypsies (CCIT)
41. International Catholic Committee of Nurses and Medical Social Assistants (CICIAMS)
42. International Catholic Conference of Guiding (ICCG)
43. International Catholic Conference of Scouting (ICCS)
44. International Catholic Migration Commission (ICMC)
45. International Catholic Movement for Intellectual and Cultural Affairs (ICMICA-Pax Romana)
46. International Catholic Rural Association (ICRA)

47. International Catholic Society for Girls (ACISJF)
48. International Catholic Union of the Press (UCIP)
49. International Christian Union of Business Executives (UNIAPAC)
50. International Confederation of Professional Associations of Domestic Workers (IAG)
51. International Confederation of the Volunteers of Suffering Centers (International Confederation CVS)
52. International Coordination of Young Christian Workers (ICYCW)
53. International Council of Catholic Men (FIHC-Unum Omnes)
54. International Federation of Catholic Associations of the Blind (FIDACA)
55. International Federation of Catholic Medical Associations (FIAMC)
56. International Federation of Catholic Parochial Youth Movements (FIMCAP)
57. International Federation of Catholic Pharmacists (FIPC)
58. International Federation of Catholic Universities (IFCU)
59. International Federation of L'Arche Communities (L'Arche International)
60. International Federation of Pueri Cantores (FIPC)
61. International Federation of Rural Adult Catholic Movements (FIMARC)
62. International Forum of Catholic Action (IFCA)
63. International Independent Christian Youth (JICI)
64. International Kolping Society (IKS)
65. International Military Apostolate (AMI)
67. International Movement of Apostolate in the Independent Social Milieus (MIAMSI)

68. International Movement of Catholic Agricultural and Rural Youth (MIJARC)
69. International Movement of Catholic Students (IMCS-Pax Romana)
70. International Movement of the Apostolate for Children (MIDADE)
71. International Union of Catholic Esperantists (IKUE)
72. International Union of Catholic Jurists (UIJC)
73. International Union of European Guides and Scouts – European Scouting Federation (UIGSE-FSE)
74. International Young Catholic Students (IYCS)
75. Lay Claretian Movement (MSC)
76. Legion of Mary
77. Life Ascending International (VMI)
78. Light-Life Movement (RŚŻ)
79. 'Living In' Spirituality Movement
80. Marianist Lay Communities (MLC)
81. Memores Domini Lay Association (Memores Domini)
82. Militia Christi (MJC)
83. Militia of the Immaculata (MI)
84. Missionary Community of Villaregia (CMV)
85. Missionary Contemplative Movement 'P. de Foucauld'
86. Oasis Movement
87. Pope John XXIII Community Association
88. Prayer and Life Workshops (TOV)
89. 'Pro Deo et Fratribus – Famiglia di Maria' Association (PDF-FM)
90. Promoting Group of the Movement for a Better World (PG of the MBW)
91. Regnum Christi Apostolic Movement
92. Salesian Cooperators Association (ACS)
93. Salesian Youth Movement (SYM)

94. Sanguis Christi Union (USC)
95. Sant'Egidio Community
96. Schoenstatt Women's Apostolic Union
97. School of the Cross
98. Secular Missionary Carmel (CMS)
99. Seguimi Lay Group of Human-Christian Promotion
100. Sermig
101. Shalom Catholic Community
102. Silent Workers of the Cross Association (SODC)
103. Society of St Vincent de Paul (SSVP)
104. St Benedict Patron of Europe Association (ASBPE)
105. St Francis de Sales Association
106. Teams of Our Lady (Equipes Notre Dame)
107. Teresian Apostolic Movement (TAM)
108. Teresian Association (TA)
109. Union of Catholic Apostolate (UAC)
110. Work of Mary (Focolare Movement)
111. Work of Nazareth (ODN)
112. Work of Saint John of Avila
113. Work of Saint Teresa
114. World Catholic Association for Communication
115. World Confederation of the Past Pupils of Mary Help of Christians
116. World Federation of Nocturnal Adoration Societies
117. World Movement of Christian Workers (WMCW)
118. World Organisation of Former Pupils of Catholic Education (OMAEC)
119. World Organisation of the Cursillo Movement (OMCC)
120. World Union of Catholic Teachers (WUCT)
121. World Union of Catholic Women's Organisations (WUCWO)
122. Worldwide Marriage Encounter (WWME)

# ⟹ Acknowledgements ⟸

I WOULD LIKE TO ACKNOWLEDGE WITH GRATITUDE the great work of all at Veritas, in particular Donna Doherty for her guidance and encouragement, Caitríona Clarke and Emma O'Donoghue for their managerial and editing work, and Marie O'Neill for her diligence in marketing.

I sincerely thank the wonderful people from the ten movements named in this book who were willing to share their stories with me and who made me so very welcome at their meetings and in their homes. Thanks too to Fr Gerard Moloney CSsR, editor at Redemptorist Communications, who commissioned the original articles for *Reality* magazine.

Thanks to my friends who read the initial drafts and provided me with invaluable feedback, in particular Brendan Purcell, Brendan Leahy, and Anne Marie Foley.

Finally, a huge thank you to my family, especially to my husband, Aidan, who is a tower of strength and always so supportive.